MAINTENANCE AND UPGRADES MANUAL

Land Rover
Series II, IIA and III

MAINTENANCE AND UPGRADES MANUAL

Land Rover
Series II, IIA and III

Richard Hall

THE CROWOOD PRESS

First published in 2016 by
The Crowood Press Ltd
Ramsbury, Marlborough
Wiltshire SN8 2HR

www.crowood.com

This impression 2018

British Library Cataloguing-in-Publication Data
A catalogue record for this book is available from the British Library.

ISBN 978 1 78500 135 2

Disclaimer
Safety is of the utmost importance in every aspect of an automotive workshop. The practical
procedures and the tools and equipment used in automotive workshops are potentially
dangerous. Tools should be used in strict accordance with the manufacturer's recommended
procedures and current health and safety regulations. The author and publisher cannot accept
responsibility for any accident or injury caused by following the advice given in this book.

Typeset by Jean Cussons Typesetting, Diss, Norfolk

Printed and bound in India by Replika Press Pvt. Ltd

contents

The classic Land Rover: 1964 Series IIA hard top, freshly restored in Marine Blue.

introduction and model history

Between 1958 and 1985, more than a million Series II, IIA and III Land Rovers rolled out of the Solihull factory. Simple, rugged and durable, they have survived in very large numbers and many are still working hard for a living in almost every country in the world. But with the oldest survivors fast approaching their sixtieth birthday, the vehicles are now rightly regarded as true classics to be cherished and admired. The aims of this book are to help you to select the Series II, IIA or III Land Rover that is right for you, to keep it running the way Solihull intended and, perhaps, to upgrade and modify it to make it more usable in modern traffic conditions. You will also learn how even the most battered and neglected old Land Rover can be restored to its former glory.

The first vehicles to bear the Land Rover badge appeared in 1948, and the range that was produced between 1948 and 1958 is now known retrospectively as 'Series One'. The vehicle was conceived as a stop-gap model for the Rover car company in the austerity years that followed the Second World War. Materials of all kinds, and especially steel, were in short supply, and car manufacturers producing vehicles for export markets tended to be favoured by the Government when it came to allocating resources. Rover had little to sell other than large, luxurious saloon cars of pre-war design. The company needed a new product, and fast.

And so the Series One was born. Intended to supplant the cast-off wartime Jeeps that had proved so popular across the world, the new model was built along very much the same lines as the Jeep: separate chassis, strong solid axles mounted on leaf springs, four-wheel drive, plenty of ground clearance for rough terrain and the minimum of creature comforts. Rover envisaged selling just a few thousand Land Rovers to keep the factory busy until the launch of the new 'P4' saloon car, so the body shape was kept simple: mostly flat panels riveted together at right angles, requiring the minimum of costly press tools. Body-work was largely aluminium, which was easier to obtain than sheet steel. Major mechanical components, including the engine and gearbox, were 'borrowed' from other models in the Rover range.

It is fair to say that the company underestimated the demand for its new utility vehicle. Within a year, the vehicles were being snapped up as fast as Rover could build them, and users were demanding more – more power, more reliability, more comfort, more load-carrying capacity. Solihull did its best to respond with bigger engines, stronger suspension, long wheelbase and five-door Station Wagon variants, but the essential problem remained: the Series One simply was not designed for high-volume mass production or for the kind of routine overloading and rough treatment to which it was now being subjected. The company needed to do something drastic.

In March 1958, the 'Series II' Land Rover was launched. It was bigger and sturdier than the Series One, with a new petrol engine giving 50 per cent more power than the old one. It had more load-carrying space, strengthened mechanicals, better brakes and a new body shape by David Bache, Rover's in-house designer. Similar at a first glance to the Series One, the new body featured curved upper sides of much greater depth, and was so successful that the basic shape can still be seen in today's Defender. In fact, you can take the doors from a brand new Defender and bolt them onto a 1958 Series II, if you so wish.

The Series II was available from the start in both long- and short-wheelbase variants, with a choice of petrol or diesel engine. An all-new and strikingly handsome five-door Station Wagon followed a year later, its clean lines a sharp contrast to the Series One Station Wagon, which looked as though it had been pieced together using several different vehicles and a large Meccano set. The new model was an immediate success, with annual sales climbing from around 25,000 in the last full year of Series One production to 35,000 by 1961.

That year saw the introduction of a more powerful diesel engine to replace the rather feeble Series One-derived unit, and the change (along with a few minor cosmetic improvements) was considered important enough for Solihull to designate the new model 'Series IIA'. Sales continued to increase, helped by the addition to the range of a more powerful 6-cylinder engine option in 1967, and a round of modest (but welcome) improvements to the interior and electrical systems in the same year. In 1969, the headlights were moved out to the front wings to comply with new legislation, but further changes were just around the corner.

By the late sixties, Rover was running into problems. In overseas markets, the Toyota Land Cruiser was starting to eat away at Series IIA sales. Like the original Land Rover, the Toyota was inspired by the wartime Jeep and had many of the same attributes. It had beam axles, leaf springs, four-wheel drive and a simple, rugged construction. Its all-steel body corroded rapidly in damp climates, but in the Australian outback or the South African veldt that was of little consequence. What mattered was that it had a far more powerful engine than the Land Rover, could carry heavier loads and very rarely broke down. By 1965, Toyota had sold 50,000 'J' series Land Cruisers; in 1968, total production topped 100,000. Land Rover might still be selling three Series IIAs for every Land Cruiser, but the Japanese rival was catching up fast.

A new model was needed to replace the Series IIA, but by now political events had intervened. In 1966, Rover had merged with Leyland Motors, a successful and profitable manufacturer of heavy commercial vehicles, which already owned Rover's great car-making rival, Triumph. The Gov-

Red knob, yellow knob: astonishing off-road performance on demand.

Made in Solihull and proud of it.

ernment's policy of the time was to strongly encourage consolidation within the car industry, and so when British Motor Holdings (owners of Jaguar, Austin and Morris among others) ran into financial trouble two years later, Leyland was prevailed upon to combine with the loss-making giant to form British Leyland.

From now on, any new Land Rover product development would have to compete for limited funds with the high-volume car makers, Austin and Morris. With Series IIA sales still climbing and much of the Austin–Morris range desperately overdue for replacement, this was a competition Rover was never likely to win. To make matters worse, whatever funding was available to the Land Rover division would have to be shared with the revolutionary new Range Rover, scheduled for launch in 1970.

And so the Land Rover Series III quietly entered the market in 1971 to a distinctly lukewarm reception. It was little more than a Series IIA with a cosmetic makeover.

Handsome beast: five-door Station Wagon in side profile.

Outside it sported a moulded plastic grille panel and less obtrusive door and windscreen hinges. Inside there was a plastic dashboard with the instruments positioned in front of the driver and more modern switchgear. (Even the instruments were carried over unchanged from the Series IIA.) Underneath, Rover's engineers had managed to cram a few more components into the 1937-design gearbox, now giving synchromesh on all four forward gears. The long-wheelbase version acquired a stronger rear axle. And at that point the money must have run out: engines, suspension, steering and most of the body and interior were carried over unchanged from the old model.

'If it ain't broke...', etc. And at first the philosophy of changing as little as possible seemed to pay off. Sales continued to hold up at around the 50,000 a year mark, but by the end of the seventies it was obvious that all was far from well. In 1977, the company sold 42,000 Series IIIs; four years later that number had halved. The Series III soldiered on, largely unchanged and increasingly obsolete. But amid the gloom of power cuts, wildcat strikes and the three-day week, the engineers at Solihull were working hard to turn the Series III into the vehicle it should have been from the start. The result was the 109 V8.

The V8 (known unofficially as the 'Stage One' as it was the first part of a long-term plan to turn Land Rover's fortunes around) was a fine example of what can be done by a small group of determined engineers working on a limited budget. They took a standard long-wheelbase Series III, reworked the chassis to take the 3.5-litre V8 engine and gearbox from the Range Rover, redesigned the front axle to cope with permanent four-wheel drive (as opposed to the part-time system of all previous Series vehicles) and moved the radiator forwards so that the front panel was flush with the wings.

Finally, Solihull had a Land Rover with power and load-hauling ability to match its rivals, and a gearbox that would stand up to any amount of abuse. The marketing department came up with a range of bright new colours (actually 'borrowed' from the Triumph sports car range) and some large 'Land Rover V8' stickers along the sides, and set out to reclaim the overseas markets that Land Rover had lost. But it was too little, too late. Sales stabilized for a while, and the new 'High Capacity Pickup' body option from 1982, with enough space to fit an 8 × 4ft board flat between the wheelarches, did a little to help stop the rot.

But all the Series III could do now was to limp along for a couple more years. The last few (military specification) vehicles left Solihull in 1985. At the time, few mourned the end of the traditional leaf-sprung Land Rover because by now the extensively redesigned Ninety and One Ten were in full production, arguably ten years later than they should have been, but providing a far more comfortable and usable vehicle for the diminishing number of customers who had not already been lost to Land Rover's Japanese rivals. Did anyone then imagine that thirty years later, people would be extracting beaten-up old Series III Land Rovers from barns and farmyards and restoring them to better-than-new condition?

Optional power take-off added to the versatility of these vehicles.

The mighty V8: a very early 109 V8 soft top in Masai Red.

Enter the Series III: here we have one of the first off the production line, bristling with dealer-fitted options, including capstan winch and rear-mounted power take-off.

Timeline: Series II, IIA and III, 1958–85

1958	Series II launched
1959	2286cc petrol engine now available in 88in models. Five-door Station Wagon introduced.
1960	Aluminium underseat tool locker replaced with steel.
1961	Series IIA launched with new 2286cc diesel engine option and minor electrical changes.
1962	Headlamps now mounted flush with grille panel. Flat front valance replaced with curved one.
1967	Dashboard redesigned with new switchgear and single wiper motor. Solid-spoke steering wheel instead of sprung-spoke, 2625cc petrol engine option, Zenith carburettor replaced Solex on 2286cc petrol engine.
1969	Headlamps moved out to the front wings. Shallower side sills.
1971	Series III launched – new dashboard, all synchromesh gearbox, stronger rear axle on 109in models.
1979	109 V8 launched.
1980	New five-bearing engine block for 2286cc models. Larger front brakes on 88in vehicles.
1981	2625cc engine option discontinued.
1982	High Capacity Pickup launched. Station Wagons now available in 'County' trim.
1983	Civilian production of 109in vehicles ended, replaced by new One Ten.
1984	Production of 88in vehicles ended, replaced by new Ninety.
1985	The last military 109in vehicles left the production line.

Main dimensions for 4-cylinder petrol vehicles, taken from the Series III owner's manual (1978 edition) – weights for earlier and later models, and variants with different engines, may vary slightly

	88in Regular	88in Station Wagon	109in Regular	109in Station Wagon
Length (mm)	3,620	3,620	4,440	4,440
Width (mm)	1,680	1,680	1,680	1,680
Height (mm)	1,950	1,980	2,060	2,070
Weight (kg)	1,339	1,488	1,497	1,702
Payload (kg)	454 (1)	45 (2)	908 (1)	181 (3)
Floor length (mm)	1,206	–	1,850	–
Floor width (mm)	921	–	921	–

(1) Plus driver and two passengers.
(2) Plus driver and six passengers.
(3) Plus driver and nine passengers.

Series IIA hard top from 1964 in very clean, original condition.

2 *choosing your Land Rover*

Series II, IIA and III Land Rovers were available in a large number of different configurations and the complexity of the range can seem baffling to the novice. Long or short wheelbase, petrol or diesel, hard top, soft top, truck cab, Station Wagon – each model was built to do a different job, and in choosing your vehicle you must first ask yourself what job you want it to do for you. This chapter will guide you through the main options.

Series III five-door Station Wagon in Limestone.

LONG VERSUS SHORT WHEELBASE

These vehicles come in two lengths: short wheelbase or '88' (88in between axle centres); and long wheelbase or '109' (109in between axle centres). The 109 obviously has far more room in the back than the 88, which will just about cope with a couple of small straw bales. It also has more room for the driver as the seat can be moved further back: an 88 can be very cramped for anyone above average height. A 109 is a fair bit heavier than an 88, accelerates more slowly, uses more fuel and has a much larger turning circle, which can make manoeuvring difficult in crowded car parks. On the other hand, the ride is far less choppy and if you need forward-facing seats in the back to accommodate young children, only a 109 (in Station Wagon form) will provide this as standard. 4-cylinder engines were available across the range throughout the production run, but 6-cylinder and V8 engines were only offered in 109in variants.

PETROL VERSUS DIESEL

The vast majority of these vehicles left the factory with 4-cylinder engines of 2286cc capacity (widely referred to as the 'two and a quarter') in either petrol or diesel form. The

The 2-litre engine from the Series One was carried over for the first few months of Series II 88in production.

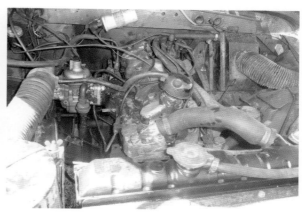

A 6-cylinder engine was an option from 1967 onwards.

two engines are closely related and share many common components, but have many different characteristics. Far more petrol-engined vehicles were built than diesels, and with good reason. The petrol engine is quieter, smoother and substantially more powerful than the diesel. It requires less frequent oil changes, starts more readily in cold weather and the difference in fuel economy is less than you might expect.

An 88 with a petrol engine in good order should average around 18–20mpg (14–16ltr/100km). For the same vehicle with the diesel engine you might see 23–25mpg (11–12ltr/100km). As for performance, the petrol vehicle in standard form will happily cruise at 55mph (88km/h) without losing too much speed on hills. The diesel starts to become unhappy and flustered above 45mph (72km/h) and even a moderate gradient will quickly see you having to

drop down through the gears. But the diesel has a growly, no-nonsense character all of its own, and many people are happy to tolerate its weaknesses for this reason. If you cannot make up your mind, try to drive good examples of both and see which you prefer.

Other, less common engine options that you might find are:

◆ 2052cc diesel, Series II, 1958–61. Now very rare and for good reason. Inadequately developed, unreliable and with abysmal performance, best left to serious collectors.
◆ 1997cc petrol, Series II, 88in, 1958 only. For the first few months of production the short-wheelbase petrol Series II used an engine carried over from the Series One. Now quite rare, rather poorer performance than the 1959-on vehicles, and parts can be hard to find.

The V8 engine is a tight fit in the Series III engine bay, but access for servicing is still good.

◆ 2625cc petrol, Series IIA/III, 1967–81. Silky smooth 6-cylinder engine taken from Rover's saloon car range. Makes a lovely noise, but performance is not that much better than the standard 4-cylinder engine and the fuel consumption is significantly worse. Many parts, including water pumps, are now almost impossible to obtain new.

◆ 3528cc petrol, Series III, 109 V8, 1979–84. The legendary Rover V8, strangled to a feeble 91bhp in the Series III to avoid overwhelming the brakes. Removal of the intake restrictors is not difficult and increases power to a more respectable 134bhp, which is plenty. Rather thirsty, typically 15–17mpg (17–19ltr/100km) on a run but consumption can drop into single figures around town. More complex to service and maintain than the 2286cc 'fours', and expensive to rebuild when worn out.

Engine Conversions Over the years, just about every engine that will physically fit has been dropped into the engine bay of a 'Series' Land Rover. Some of these conversions are very good (notably the 200TDi engine from the Discovery), others less so. Parts availability for older non-Land Rover engines can be a nightmare and some conversions have been very amateurishly done, the result being unreliable or even dangerous. For the first-time buyer, the safest advice is to choose a vehicle that retains the type of engine with which it left the factory.

MAIN BODY TYPES

Hard Top A van-type upper body, with one door on each side and either a sideways opening rear door ('safari door') or split, two-piece tailgate, hinged top and bottom ('catflap'). The plain side-panels can readily be fitted with windows to improve visibility. Probably the most common body type.

Soft Top Full-length canvas roof supported on a steel frame, with a roll-up rear panel and drop-down tailgate. Canvas can be removed for summer use but is secured with very many ropes and straps: not a two-minute job to refit when it starts to rain. Replacement canvases are available with clear vinyl side-windows and/or sides that roll up. Draughty, noisy, minimal security and prone to water leaks, but very much in the spirit of the 'classic' Land Rover, and fun.

Engine specifications for Series II/IIA and III vehicles				
Fuel	Capacity (cc)	Cylinders	Power (bhp)	Torque (lb ft)
Petrol	1997	4	52	101
Petrol	2286	4	74	120
Petrol	2625	6	86	132
Petrol	3528	8	91	166
Diesel	2052	4	51	87
Diesel	2286	4	62	103

1966 Series IIA 109in hard top, showing 'catflap' upper tailgate.

1960 Series II soft top fresh from a major restoration.

Canvas tops are available in a variety of colours: this one has the optional side-windows.

Still working for a living: 1965 Series IIA 109in truck cab in rural surroundings.

Truck Cab Pickup-type detachable cab with curved corner windows to improve visibility. Snug in winter, as the heater has less work to do. Often seen in conjunction with a canvas rear roof, similar to the full-length soft top but stopping just short of the back of the truck cab and known as a 'three-quarter' canvas. Much favoured by farmers in days gone by.

88in Station Wagon Similar to hard top but with sliding side-windows, a double-skinned 'tropical' roof with opening air-vents and small 'alpine light' windows, and four inward-facing rear seats. Early 88 Station Wagons are quite rare, later Series III vehicles more common. Factory-built Station Wagons with diesel engines are (at the time of writing) exempt from the London Low Emission Zone. Rear seats are uncomfortable for adults and cannot safely be fitted with child seats for young children. Series III available from 1981 onwards in 'County' specification with cloth seats, additional soundproofing and tinted windows.

Truck cab and three-quarter canvas: this is actually a very late Series IIA sporting a Series III plastic grille. Windscreen hinges reveal its true identity.

Series IIA 88in Station Wagons are quite rare. This is a shabby but remarkably original example.

Note the double-skinned 'tropical' roof and sliding side-windows.

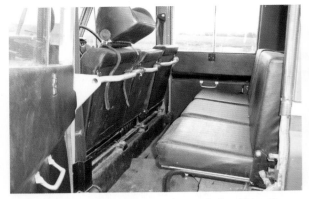

Second-row seats on a Station Wagon – better suited to children than adults.

The original people carrier: room for six more in the back of this five-door Station Wagon.

109in Station Wagon Five doors and forward-facing second-row seats, either three individual forward-folding seats or (more rarely) a single bench seat. In-ward-facing bench seats in the back, giving seating for either ten or twelve people. The two outer second-row seats can be fitted with three-point seat belts, allowing child seats to be used. Complex and rot-prone body structure, expensive to restore if in poor condition. Like the 88 Station Wagon, late Series III available in County specification.

109in High Capacity Pickup Introduced very late in the Series III production run and not a huge seller. Truck cab and separate pickup-style rear body, giving a load space wider and longer than the standard 109 and a full-width tailgate. These vehicles were aimed at serious commercial users and tended to have a very hard life; survivors in good condition are rare.

88in Airportable ('Lightweight') Developed for mili-tary use with a narrower, very angular body and detach-able panels. Supplied to the British Army in large numbers

and many have survived in civilian hands. Running gear is mostly standard Series IIA/III, most vehicles have full soft-top. Doors always fit poorly due to a design fault. Light-weights are crude, draughty, noisy and impossible to keep free of rainwater leaks but, as a 'fun' Land Rover for summer use, they are hard to beat.

Ex-Gulf War Lightweight: everything painted sand colour, even the handbrake.

Series III Lightweight: minimalist fun.

MILITARY LAND ROVERS

The Ministry of Defence purchased large numbers of Series II, IIA and III Land Rovers, with the last few leaving military service in 1993. As well as the 'Lightweight', many thousands of 88s and 109s were built for military use. The early vehicles were very similar to civilian vehicles, but as the Army's requirements evolved, they became progressively more specialized. Here are some of the key features you might find on an ex-military Series vehicle:

- *Twin underseat fuel tanks with filler cap accessed by lifting the seat base.*
- *Shallow rear crossmember with mounting points for a NATO tow hitch.*
- *Six-way lighting switch with provision for 'convoy lights' (small lights mounted under the vehicle, allowing convoys to creep around at night with no lights showing).*
- *'Combat' chassis on 109in vehicles, with deeper spring hangers and extended shackles to increase ground clearance.*
- *Oil cooler mounted in front of the radiator.*
- *24V electrical system on Fitted for Radio (FFR) vehicles, with a large generator mounted high up in the engine bay, and fully screened ignition components.*
- *Military-style lights with screw-in lenses on side, tail and indicator lights, quick-release headlight units without trim rings.*
- *Heavy-duty double-height front bumper.*

Many ex-military vehicles will have been 'civilianized' to some extent: rear crossmembers are often replaced with civilian-pattern ones to allow the fitting of a standard tow hitch, 24V vehicles converted to conventional 12V systems, and military light units replaced with cheaper standard items. Ex-military vehicles that still retain all their original features are quite rare and have a strong enthusiast following.

Military indicator light unit with screw-in glass lens.

Some Series IIIs lasted long enough in Army service to receive these plastic lenses in place of glass ones.

Factory-fitted oil cooler normally found on military vehicles.

SERIES II, IIA OR III?

Although the fundamentals of the design changed little through its twenty-seven-year production life, there was a steady process of mechanical refinement and cosmetic tweaking. Many Land Rover enthusiasts feel that the Series III, with its plastic dashboard, lost much of the period charm of the earlier vehicles, and prices tend to reflect this. However, later (post-1980) Series IIIs featured a number of very welcome mechanical improvements, including stronger

five-bearing engines, more robust gearboxes, servo-assisted split-circuit brakes across the range, and larger front brakes on the 88in model. Many earlier vehicles have been retro-fitted with some or all of these features, but even an original, unmodified Series II will cope far more happily with modern traffic conditions than most family saloon cars of the same era.

Build quality on earlier vehicles was undeniably better than those produced in the British Leyland era, and later Series IIIs often have far more rust in the chassis and

Typical Series IIA interior with most of its original features and that 'lived-in' look.

Series IIAs from 1967 onwards had the instrument panel painted black. The large knob below the panel is a hand throttle, which was standard on diesels.

Plastic radiator grille on a Series III in Pastel Green – one of the less common factory colours.

bulkhead than vehicles built twenty years earlier. However, with even the youngest examples now thirty years old, the age of a vehicle will be of little relevance in determining its condition. Almost all these vehicles will by now have had a great deal of repair and refurbishment work to keep them on the road.

So, in deciding whether to opt for a Series II, IIA or III, you need to consider how much you can afford to spend, and whether there are particular design features that you absolutely must have. All Series II/IIA models had an all-metal dash panel with instruments in the middle; models up to 1969 had the headlamps in the centre panel, which people tend to regard as the 'classic' Series Land Rover look. Series IIAs from 1967 onwards gained a much more effective windscreen-wiper system with a single in-dash motor replacing the twin screen-mounted motors of the earlier vehicles. So, arguably the most desirable combination of virtues can be found in those Series IIAs produced between 1967 and 1969. This, however, is a matter of personal preference.

Another factor that may influence your choice is the question of exemption from road tax and MoT. At the time of writing, vehicles built before 31 December 1974 are classed as 'Historic Vehicles' with no road tax payable. The cut-off point was frozen for many years, but the Government has recently moved it onto a rolling basis, so that newer vehicles will, at some future point, become eligible for the zero tax rate. Those built before 31 December 1959 are exempt from the requirement for a compulsory annual MoT test but this concession has met with a luke-warm response: a lot can go wrong with an old vehicle in the space of a year, and owners of pre-1960 vehicles are well advised to continue having their vehicles tested annually.

The appeal of tax-exempt status is easy to see, but tax-exempt vehicles attract a significant price premium over later ones, and by restricting yourself to pre-1975 vehicles you will be significantly limiting the choice available to you. To pass over a good 1981 Series III in favour of a ropey 1973 one is madness: the older vehicle will cost you far more in repair and maintenance costs than you will save in road tax.

Last of the line: a very late (1984) Series III 88in hard top.

OPTIONAL EQUIPMENT

Totally original, unmodified old Land Rovers are very rare. Almost all will have been customized in some way to suit the taste of the previous owner(s), and these features may be worth paying a premium for. Probably the most desir-

able option is an overdrive unit. All these vehicles had a four-speed gearbox with low gearing for heavy towing, and tend to become noisy and stressed at higher speeds. An overdrive is a two-speed gearbox bolted to the back of the main transmission, operated by a lever in the cab. When engaged, it reduces engine revolutions by about a quarter,

High-back seats and moulded floor mats help to make this 1960 Series II fit for everyday use.

Series III interior: this one has high back seats and door trims.

CENTRE LEFT: County Station Wagons had cloth covered seats.

CENTRE RIGHT: Rear bench seats and side-window canvas in a Series II soft top.

Power take-off drive is a rare accessory for which few people have any practical use.

This 88in Station Wagon is one of a batch purchased by Post Office Telephones and all registered SYF...F.

giving a far more relaxed cruise and better fuel economy. Overdrives are highly desirable, expensive to buy new and not easy to find second-hand.

Improvements to interior comfort are also welcome. The seats fitted as standard to the majority of Series II, IIA and III vehicles are square slabs of padded black vinyl with no headrests, no lower back or lateral support and little (if any) facility for adjustment. High-back seats with headrests are quite common and make a big difference on a long journey, but beware of vehicles that have been fitted with car-type seats. The seat base on a 'Series' Land Rover is very shallow, and incorrectly dimensioned replacement seats will leave your thighs jammed against the bottom of the steering wheel and your eyes in line with the top of the windscreen frame.

A front-mounted winch, whether of the old-fashioned capstan-type or more modern drum-type, is only worth paying for if you actually intend to use it. Cosmetic 'enhancements', such as chequer-plate protection panels, flared wheelarches and fancy paint, tend to make a vehicle worth less, not more. Big, wide, off-road tyres can be very noisy, increase the turning circle, make the steering much heavier and spoil the ride and handling on-road. And a

high-level snorkel air intake is only of any use if the rest of the vehicle has been thoroughly waterproofed as well.

Having decided which model(s) to look at, and worked out how much you can afford to spend, you can now go out and look at a few. The next chapter will tell you what to look for.

The four-wheel drive Station Wagon badge is often missing.

viewing and buying your Land Rover

Old Land Rovers are everywhere. There are hundreds, maybe thousands for sale at any one time. You can find them advertised in the back of Land Rover magazines, on car sales websites such as Car and Classic, and auction websites such as eBay. Specialist dealers sometimes have a couple for sale alongside more modern Defenders and Range Rovers. You may be driving through the countryside and come across one parked at the roadside with a home-made 'For Sale' sign attached to it. The websites of Land Rover clubs, such as the Series Two Club, are another good place to look.

The first thing to remember is that if someone is selling a Series II, IIA or III, it is for a reason and the seller may not be honest with you about the reason. Selling an old vehicle seems to bring out the worst in people. The second thing to remember is that not all sellers are knowledgeable about their own vehicles: 'good condition, drives well' may be a view honestly held by the seller, but it is not necessarily an accurate one. So believe nothing you are told, unless it is backed up with documentary proof; trust instead your own eyes, ears and instincts.

You will need a torch, a pair of overalls, a screwdriver or small hammer and a large plastic sheet to cover the ground while you crawl underneath. A pen and notebook are useful, so that you can make a note of defects as you go along. If you have a smartphone, you can use the DVLA website to check the vehicle's details and the validity of the MoT certificate and registration document (V5). You need to allow yourself plenty of time – at least an hour – to carry out a thorough inspection and road test. And above all, you need the right attitude. Be prepared to ask direct questions, and do not under any circumstances allow yourself to fall in love with the vehicle you are looking at. These vehicles were built in huge numbers: the one you are looking at is not the only one you will ever find.

Typical rot along the bottom of the door frame. Replacement doors are inexpensive.

Typically shabby engine bay in a 2.25 petrol Series IIA.

This rear spring hanger looks solid enough until poked with a screwdriver.

The inner face of the rear crossmember can only be checked from underneath.

First things first: take a walk around the vehicle and look at it from all angles. Does it sit straight and level? Do the doors and wings fit properly? Is there any obvious body damage? First impressions count for a lot: a straight, honest and well-loved vehicle will shout out its virtues to you. Open the bonnet: is the engine covered in filthy old oil? Is it warm, having been run up before you arrived to hide a cold-starting issue? Now put on your overalls, lay out the ground-sheet and prepare to get dirty.

Chassis This is the backbone of any 'Series' Land Rover and almost every vehicle you look at will have had some welded repairs over the years. Inspect every inch of it: you are looking for rust holes, bulging and crumbling metal and badly welded patch repairs. Hollow box sections (of which there are many) should ring when lightly tapped: a dull thud may indicate problems. Thick, rubbery underseal could be hiding all manner of evil and it is unlikely that the seller will let you peel it away to see what lies underneath.

Pay particular attention to the front chassis legs where the springs and front bumper attach; the outriggers, which support the base of the door pillars; the mountings (and outriggers on a 109), which attach the rear springs to the chassis; and the rear crossmember, especially around the area in the centre where the tow hitch bolts through. The MoT test specifies that a vehicle will fail if the structure is weakened by corrosion within 30cm (12in) of a suspension, steering or body mounting point, or within 30cm (12in) of the tow hitch (if fitted). On five-door Station Wagons, inspect the sill rails that run below the doors from front to rear, the base of the

pillars for the second-row doors and the angled section at the rear edge of the second-row doors that supports the door catch. Significant rot in any of these areas will be expensive to rectify.

Rotten bulkhead outriggers are common, although not usually as bad as this one.

This bulkhead outrigger has had a patch welded to the underside. Check the metal all around the patch.

Bulkhead Another structurally critical component that supports much of the bodywork and carries loads from the steering system, brake pedal and seatbelts. The same MoT rules apply as for the chassis, meaning that corrosion almost anywhere within the bulkhead structure will constitute an MoT fail. Footwells will often have been replaced or patched – check that any repair sections have been welded all round, not just riveted and painted over. The mounting feet at the base of the door pillars can corrode away and are very hard to replace. Upper corners around the top door hinge are another common rot spot, and rust in this area is often hidden with plastic filler – look carefully for cracks and sanding marks in the surface and be very suspicious of any bulging metal or fresh shiny paint.

Evidence of rot at the base of the door pillar on a Series IIA. Has it eaten into the mounting foot? You need to check.

The rust hole is obvious enough, but what lies beneath the bubbling paint next to it?

Original footwell (note pressed ribs) with no sign of welded repairs, but rust starting to form where water has leaked in.

Top inner corners of the bulkhead can be hard to repair: this one is fine.

Upper front corner of bulkhead: original spot welds still visible, so you can be sure there is no plastic filler here. This is as good as you will find.

Suspension While underneath the vehicle, take a good look at the leaf springs. Rust builds up between the leaves, causing them to spread apart, distort and eventually break. The shock absorbers should be free from oily deposits and securely mounted top and bottom, with no free play in the rubber bushes. The bump stops (rectangular rubber blocks above the axles) should be intact, not missing or hanging off, and the section of chassis to which they are bolted should be free from holes or bulging rusty metal.

Axles The rear axle on most 88s and older 109s has a hollow box-section strengthening member underneath, which can rust from the inside out and should be inspected carefully. Axle casings should be free from serious corrosion and obvious impact damage. At the front there are two large chrome balls with a large round seal bearing against them: if the chrome is badly pitted with corrosion, the seals

will become damaged, allowing the oil to leak out. This is very expensive to repair. The outer lip of the brake drums should be dry with no evidence of oil or brake fluid leaks inside the drums.

Exhaust System This is a simple affair, suspended from square rubber strap-type mounts. Any corrosion or holes should be obvious. Check the mounting brackets on the chassis, as they can corrode. New exhaust systems for these vehicles are inexpensive and not too hard to fit, but a badly deteriorated exhaust can be a useful bargaining point.

Oil Leaks All old Land Rovers leak oil. There is a saying in Land Rover circles that if it doesn't leak oil, that is because it is empty and needs topping up. There is some truth in this. Most oil leaks are fairly easy to rectify: leaks from the gearbox drive or differential drive flanges can usually be

This steering swivel has some slight pitting to the chrome and is damp with oil, but should have a few years' life left.

This one has no chrome plating left at all and is scrap.

sorted by replacing the seals. Gearboxes invariably leak oil from around the selector mechanism at the top: this runs down the sides of the casing and drips from the bottom. Engines tend to be fairly oily underneath, with oil leaking out of every joint and gasket from the oil filler cap downwards.

However there are a couple of leaks that are more serious and harder to deal with. Oil on the outside of the axle casing may result from a rust hole or off-roading damage: this usually requires the oil pan to be cut out and a new one welded in. Oil dripping from around the join between the engine and gearbox is most likely to be due to a failed rear crankshaft oil seal. Replacement is an engine-out job, and the clutch will probably be contaminated with oil too. Engines quite often leak oil from the front seal as well: to replace this the front pulley, water pump and timing cover will need to come off. So be very wary of significant oil leaks from either the front or back of the engine, as these are expensive to repair.

Inside the Engine Bay   There is only a certain amount you can learn by looking in here, especially if you are unfamiliar with these vehicles. Check the oil level with the dipstick: it should be somewhere between the minimum and maximum marks and not too dirty or treacly. Very low or filthy oil suggests neglect. Remove the oil filler cap and look inside: a build-up of creamy white sludge points to a failing head-gasket or cracked cylinder head. Remove the radiator cap (very carefully using a thick cloth over it to protect your hand, especially if the engine is warm): coolant should be clean and coloured blue, green or red, indicating the presence of antifreeze. Plain water, rusty brown water or a very low coolant level are all warning signs.

Take a good look at the parts of the wiring loom that are visible within the engine bay. 'Repairs' using terminal blocks, Scotchlocks, crimped plastic connectors, random lengths of wire and sticky tape are quite common on older vehicles and will invariably give trouble in future. The

wiring loom should be securely fastened to the bodywork with the appropriate clips, not hanging loose or tied up with string. The battery should be of an appropriate size and securely clamped in position, with the leads and terminals in good order. A filthy, ancient-looking battery, with the terminals covered in crusty white deposits, will probably not have much life left in it.

Start It Up   Switch on the ignition and check that the charge and oil pressure warning lights illuminate. If not, they may have been disabled to hide a fault. Petrol engines should start readily, using the choke if cold. Diesels will normally require about 10–15 seconds of preheating using the glow plugs – much more than this may indicate worn pistons and bores. The oil pressure light should go out within a couple of seconds and any rattling noises should cease as soon as it does. A puff of blue smoke on startup is normal with petrol engines, but once running, there should be no smoke either at idle or when revved. Diesels will almost always run roughly and belch out clouds of dense blue-grey smoke when cold: if this clears within a couple of minutes, it is nothing much to worry about.

On the Road   If you have not driven one of these vehicles before, you will be in for a shock. Vague steering, heavy brakes, a hard ride and a tendency to wander across the road are all perfectly normal for the breed. But there are a few things that even the novice should be able to spot. The brakes should pull up in a straight line without excessive pedal travel. The steering should self-centre when exiting a corner – if you have to wind the wheel back to the straight-ahead position, this probably means a seized steering relay, which is seldom an easy job to replace. The clutch should not slip under load or judder when moving off from a standstill. The gearbox will probably whine under load but should not rattle or jump out of gear. And the engine should pull smoothly without spluttering or misfiring, and have enough performance to keep out of other road users' way (although the diesels can be a little marginal in this respect).

Doing the Deal   Once you have satisfied yourself that you have found a suitable vehicle, all that remains is to negotiate the purchase price. These vehicles can be difficult to value: so much depends on the exact specification and condition. Values, especially for Series II and IIA Land Rovers, have increased significantly in recent years, and the days of being able to buy a good, usable vehicle for £1,000 or less are over. At the time of writing, solid but tatty Series IIIs fetch around £2,000, similar Series IIs and IIAs £3,000, with prices for better vehicles then rising rapidly, and rebuilt or very original, unmolested examples frequently changing hands for £8,000 or more. It is worth looking at advertisements for vehicles similar to the one you are looking to buy, to get a feel for whether the price being asked is a fair one. But before you hand over the money, there is one more question you really need to ask: is the vehicle what it is claimed to be? This thorny topic is covered in the next chapter.

Free-wheeling hubs are a popular option on Series vehicles. Check that the mechanism operates smoothly.

identity issues

Buyer beware! Some old Land Rovers are not what they appear to be. The introduction of the 'historic' category for Vehicle Excise Duty gave unscrupulous owners a very strong financial incentive to transfer the identity of rusted-out old Land Rovers onto newer ones, and sadly there are a fair few vehicles out there that have had their identity tampered with to save money on road tax. Criminals hide the true identity of stolen vehicles in the same way. The Meccano-like nature of an old Land Rover means that there are also vehicles on the road that have been built up from an assortment of parts salvaged from perhaps three or four different vehicles. Your aim should be to purchase a vehicle whose legitimate identity is beyond doubt: but how to do this?

Series II, IIA and III Land Rovers left the factory with their chassis number or vehicle identification number (VIN) marked in two places. The number was stamped onto the offside front chassis leg, on the outside face above the front spring hanger, and also appeared on a stamped aluminium plate attached to the body. This plate, if present, can usually be found inside the cab (either on the firewall or in front of the driver) on vehicles up to around 1974, and inside the engine bay, either attached to the radiator support panel (1974–9) or the bulkhead (1979+). The plate is attached by screws, and the stamped chassis number is in an area that often corrodes and is patched over: this is what makes it so easy to mess around with vehicle identities. Some people do not even bother to conceal the stamped chassis number, and the author has seen a few vehicles over the years where the number on the chassis (clearly visible) does not match that on the plate.

Chassis plate on most vehicles up to 1974 is attached to the firewall in front of the gear lever.

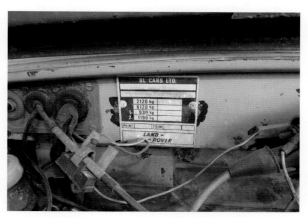

British Leyland chassis plate on 1979-onwards Series III – mounted on the front face of the bulkhead inside the engine bay.

Chassis number is – just – visible on this offside front spring hanger.

COMMON CHASSIS NUMBER PREFIXES 1958–79, UK MARKET VEHICLES

141	Series II 88in petrol
146	Series II 88in diesel
151	Series II 109in petrol
156	Series II 109in diesel
161	Series II 109in petrol Station Wagon
166	Series II 109in diesel Station Wagon
236	Series IIA 88in petrol Airportable ('Lightweight')
241	Series IIA 88in petrol
251	Series IIA 109in petrol
261	Series IIA 109in petrol Station Wagon
271	Series IIA 88in diesel
276	Series IIA 109in diesel
281	Series IIA 109in diesel Station Wagon
315	Series IIA 88in petrol Station Wagon
320	Series IIA 88in diesel Station Wagon
345	Series IIA 109in petrol 6-cylinder
350	Series IIA 109in petrol 6-cylinder Station Wagon
901	Series III 88in petrol
906	Series III 88in diesel
911	Series III 109in petrol
916	Series III 109in diesel
921	Series III 88in petrol Station Wagon
926	Series III 88in diesel Station Wagon
931	Series III 109in petrol Station Wagon
936	Series III 109in diesel Station Wagon
941	Series III 109in petrol 6-cylinder
946	Series III 109in petrol 6-cylinder Station Wagon
951	Series III 88in petrol Airportable ('Lightweight')

COMMON CHASSIS NUMBER PREFIXES 1979–85, UK MARKET VEHICLES

NB First three letters are always SAL:

LBAAG	Series III 88in diesel
LBAAH	Series III 88in petrol
LBABG	Series III 88in diesel Station Wagon
LBABH	Series III 88in petrol Station Wagon
LBBAH	Series III 88in petrol Airportable ('Lightweight')
LBCAG	Series III 109in diesel
LBCAH	Series III 109in petrol
LBCAP	Series III 109in petrol 6-cylinder
LBCAV	Series III 109in petrol V8
LBCHG	Series III 109in diesel High Capacity Pickup
LBCHH	Series III 109in petrol High Capacity Pickup
LBCHV	Series III 109in petrol V8 High Capacity Pickup
LBCMG	Series III 109in diesel Station Wagon
LBCMH	Series III 109in petrol Station Wagon
LBCMP	Series III 109in petrol 6-cylinder Station Wagon
LBCMV	Series III 109in petrol V8 Station Wagon

Your first step will be to decode the VIN, as this will tell you the original specification of the vehicle to which that VIN relates. Vehicles built up to 1979 had an eight-digit number, followed by a suffix letter from 1961 onwards, e.g. 24113767C. The first three digits indicate the vehicle specification. From 1979, Land Rover moved to the new international standard seventeen-digit system, with a combination of ten letters and numbers to show the build location, specification and model year, followed by a six-digit number, e.g.SALLBCAG1AA102345. If the specification does not match the vehicle you are looking at, you should be wary straight away.

All Series II and IIA vehicles were built before 1972 and are tax-exempt, so most of the tampering that takes place involves later Series IIIs being passed off as older vehicles. The different dashboard layout of the two vehicles is immediately obvious, and if you find a 'Series IIA' with a Series III-style dashboard, that ought to make you suspicious. The seller may claim that the vehicle was fitted with a Series III bulkhead to replace the rotten original. This is physically possible, but there are two other things you can check to verify this claim: the front brake hose brackets and the crossmember underneath the gearbox bellhousing. As you can see from the photographs, a Series II/IIA chassis differs very substantially in these areas from a Series III item.

Somewhat trickier to spot is a late Series III that has been given the identity of an earlier one. There are couple of easy things to check: if the vehicle has the rear number plate on the passenger side, it was almost certainly built after 1979,

Front brake hose bracket – Series II and IIA.

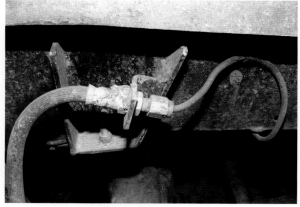

Front brake hose bracket – Series III.

Centre crossmember reinforcing gusset on Series III – shallow and angled towards the top.

The same area on a Series II/IIA chassis: the gusset is deeper, with a straight edge from top to bottom.

when the number plate was moved to make way for the mandatory rear fog-light. The same goes for a vehicle with hazard warning flashers operated by a pull switch in the upper centre of the dashboard. Dual-circuit, servo-assisted brakes were only available on most UK market vehicles from 1980 (although they can be retrofitted to earlier vehicles). Conversely, if the front face of the bulkhead has two short rain gutters, rather than one continuous full-width one, you are probably looking at a vehicle built before the end of 1973: the early design of gutter gave a lot of trouble

with water leaking into the passenger compartment and was quickly changed.

People have been building up Land Rovers from old wrecks and piles of bits for nearly as long as Land Rovers have been around. Back in the 1980s, when rotten old Range Rovers were common and coil-sprung Ninety and One Ten Land Rovers very expensive, a fair few enthusiasts put Series bodies onto cut-down Range Rover chassis, normally registering the resultant 'hybrid' using the identity from the Series body donor. The rules on such conversions

Rear view of late Series III – number plate on left, fog-light on right. 1984–85 vehicles like this one had the indicators at the lower corners of the body like a Defender.

These short, stubby rain gutters were only fitted to Series III bulkheads made before 1974.

the same wheelbase and the same leaf-spring suspension system), a chassis replacement of this type should be of no concern to VOSA and does not need to be notified. There have been several instances where well-meaning rebuilders have informed the authorities of their new replacement chassis and found themselves in a Kafkaesque tangle of bureaucracy from which there seems to be no escape.

But what of, for example, a 'Series II' that has a new galvanized chassis, all-synchromesh Series III gearbox, stronger Series III back axle and the engine from a Discovery 200TDi? Is it legal or not? The answer has to be 'it depends' – on the attitude of the VOSA inspector, his or her interpretation of the rules and the reason why the vehicle has come to VOSA's attention in the first place. It is quite rare for vehicles to be called in for inspection in this way, and if it is due to a minor anomaly in paperwork (such as the VIN number having been incorrectly recorded when the old paper records were computerized in 1974, which still causes problems on vehicles returned to the road after a long period in storage), you probably have nothing to worry about. But if your vehicle is being inspected following a fatal accident, or because it has been reported to the authorities as falsely claiming tax exemption when the only pre-1975 component is the chassis plate, you can expect to have the book thrown at you.

were substantially tightened in 1993, and it is worth taking a few moments to consider what the Vehicle and Operator Services Agency (VOSA) has to say on the subject. There are two different categories: 'rebuilt' vehicles, which will cover Land Rovers built up to near standard specification from a pile of bits; and 'radically altered' vehicles, into which category Series/Range Rover 'hybrids' fall.

For radically altered vehicles, a points system is used. A vehicle must score eight or more points to retain the original identity and avoid the need for an IVA or SVA test. The following values are allocated to the major components used:

    chassis (original or new) = 5 points
    suspension = 2 points
    axles = 2 points
    transmission = 2 points
    steering assembly = 2 points
    engine = 1 point

There is a good deal of vagueness in this and much is open to interpretation. It would appear that like-for-like replacements of major components are permitted, so a rebuilt vehicle may be fitted with a reconditioned engine, gearbox and axles without falling foul of the rules. But what is clear is that a vehicle that has been built up since 1993 (when the new rules were introduced), using either a second-hand or significantly modified chassis, should not be on the road unless it has been given an SVA or IVA test and issued with a new registration and VIN number. This applies to all 'hybrids' without exception.

Many Series vehicles have by now had the chassis replaced, often with a galvanized chassis for longevity. Provided that the replacement chassis was supplied new and is of the same pattern as the original (principally meaning

---

VOSA GUIDANCE

Rebuilt vehicles must use:

The original unmodified chassis; or a new chassis of the same specification as the original supported by evidence from the dealer or manufacturer (e.g. receipt).

And two other major components from the original vehicle – ie suspension (front & back); steering assembly; axles (both); transmission or engine.

If a second-hand chassis is used a car must pass an Individual Vehicle Approval (IVA) and light goods vans must have an enhanced single vehicle approval (ESVA) or single vehicle approval (SVA) test after which a 'Q' prefix registration number will be allocated.

maintaining your Land Rover

All the Land Rovers covered by this book were designed to be maintained in primitive conditions using mainly ordinary hand tools. There is very little that is beyond the scope of the determined home-mechanic – even the gearbox can be rebuilt in a garden shed with nothing more sophisticated than a set of feeler gauges. However, home maintenance carries a number of risks, not all of which are always fully appreciated by the would-be home-mechanic.

Working on your own vehicle is something that, if you get it wrong, could easily land you in hospital or worse. So before we start to look in detail at the various repair and maintenance procedures, please read very carefully the following Ten Commandments of Car Maintenance:

1. **Thou shalt not work underneath a vehicle with one or more wheels off the ground, unless it is securely supported on axle stands resting on a firm, flat surface.** If you crawl under a vehicle supported only by a jack, and the jack slips or fails, you stand a good chance of being crushed to death. It happens.

2. **Thou shalt not apply more force to any hand tool than it was designed to withstand.** Putting a scaffold pole over the end of a breaker bar might shift a stubborn nut; on the other hand, the bar might shatter and send splinters through your eye socket and into your brain.

3. **Thou shalt not use cutting, grinding, drilling or chiselling equipment without eye protection.** There are far too many one-eyed former home-mechanics around already and you do not want to add to their number.

4. **Thou shalt not work on safety-critical systems without first understanding how they work.** By 'safety-critical' we mainly mean brakes, steering and suspension. If you do not understand the basic mechanical principles behind, for example, a drum-brake system, leave repairing it to someone who does. You may make a bad mistake in reassembling it out of sheer ignorance. Badly fitted doors will not kill you; badly fitted brakes might.

Axle stands large and small. The large ones sit under the chassis rails; the smaller ones under the axles.

Disc cutters – the standard 4½in, and a big 9in version for serious dismantling.

5. **Thou shalt not reuse locking tabs, Nyloc nuts or other disposable locking devices.** This particularly applies to the locking tabs that secure the hub nuts. If one of these fractures due to being flattened out and bent over again, your wheel and hub will fall off. This has bad effects on straight-line stability at speed.

6. **Thou shalt beware always of asbestos dust.** It is a long time since brake and clutch linings on new vehicles contained asbestos, but it still turns up on older Land Rovers. Do not blow away the dust – spray it with water, sweep it into a plastic bag and dispose of it responsibly.

7. **Thou shalt always use a torque wrench when tightening safety-critical fasteners.** Almost every nut and bolt on a Land Rover has a factory-specified torque setting. That setting is often tighter than you might expect, and on steering and suspension components, guessing wrong could have tragic consequences.

8. **Thou shalt never work with the engine running in a confined space.** Carbon monoxide will kill you without you even realizing what is going on.

9. **Thou shalt never improvise with lifting, jacking or supporting equipment.** A Land Rover engine weighs 250kg (550lb). Use an engine crane, not a chain block slung over one of the roof timbers in your garage.

10. **Thou shalt never, ever bodge.** If you do not have the correct part or tool for the job you are doing, go out and buy it. Lashing up a temporary repair with cable ties and bits of bicycle is not an option.

LIFTING AND JACKING

These vehicles weigh between 1.4 and 1.9 tonnes, depending on specification. For safety's sake, you should aim for an overload factor of at least × 2, so your jack needs to be rated at a minimum of 2 tonnes, and axle stands at 2 tonnes per pair. For jacking, you can use either a trolley jack or hydraulic bottle jack, positioned under the axle. A trolley jack is more versatile and can simply be positioned underneath the axle differential at the lowest point. A bottle jack will need to be positioned under the axle casing towards the outer end, and there is a greater risk of it slipping than a trolley jack. First-generation Land Rover Discoveries (1989–98) came with a good-quality bottle jack with a curved top, which seats under the axle casing, and can often be acquired from vehicle breakers for very little money. Axle stands should be positioned under the plates that secure the springs to the axles, unless the springs themselves are to be removed (supporting the vehicle for spring removal is covered in Chapter 7).

It should go without saying that the vehicle should only be jacked up on firm, level ground. As soon as you lift one rear wheel off the ground, the handbrake will cease to function, as it operates on the rear propshaft rather than on each rear wheel independently. If the vehicle is on a sloping surface, it will simply roll forwards or backwards and fall off the jack. If you absolutely have to jack up the vehicle on a slope, engage four-wheel drive first. If jacking on soft ground or loose gravel, a strong wooden board at least 50mm (2in) thick should be placed under the jack and the axle stand to spread the load and provide a firm, stable surface.

TOOLS

Most of these vehicles are held together with a bewildering variety of differently sized fasteners, and you will need a fairly extensive toolkit to carry out more than basic maintenance. The main types of fastener used were:

◆ Unified National (UNC/UNF) – standard Imperial threaded fastener for the British motor industry from the mid-1950s onwards. Available in fine (UNF) and coarse (UNC)

Trolley jack behind, bottle jack from a Discovery toolkit in front.

Land Rover Special Repair Tool Number One.

threads. Spanner and socket sizes are denoted by the measurement across the flats of the nut or bolt head: so a ½in AF spanner has jaws ½in apart.

◆ British Standard (BSF/BSW) – predecessor to UNF, mainly found on major mechanical components (gearbox, axles and the 1997cc and 2625cc engines) carried over from the Series One era. BSF is fine thread, BSW coarse. BS fasteners specified a particular size of hexagonal head for each diameter of bolt: hence the size stamped on the tool bears no relation to the dimensions of the fastener it is intended to undo.

◆ Metric – from about 1980, Land Rover started a process of replacing Imperial fasteners with metric. These are mainly found on later five-bearing 2286cc engines and various body and trim components. As with UNF/UNC fasteners, the spanner size is measured across the flats.

◆ British Association (BA) – widely used for smaller screws and nuts, especially in the dashboard assembly.

There is some overlap between UN and metric spanner sizes, but almost all the BS and BA sizes fall awkwardly between the closest available UN or metric equivalent. As a minimum, you will need a socket set covering ¼–1in AF and a set of combination spanners (open jaws at one end, ring at the other) ¼–⅞in AF. A set of small BA spanners and sockets will also be very useful, and if you intend to carry out work on the gearbox or axles, this will require combination spanners and sockets in the range ⅛–½in BSW. To undo the wheel nuts, you will need either a sturdy wheel brace or a socket and breaker bar. Earlier vehicles usually have 9⁄16in BSF nuts (close enough to 24mm); post-1971 vehicles have 27mm metric nuts. To change the spark plugs on petrol engines, you will need a spark-plug socket.

Sockets come in either six- or twelve-sided versions: the six-sided have less of a tendency to round off the corners of the fastener being undone. You might also consider the very ingenious 'Metrinch' socket sets: these have a specially rounded profile and are designed so that a single socket will fit BS, UN and metric fasteners. There are four main sizes of square drive fitting for sockets: ¼, ⅜, ½ and ¾in. In general, ⅜in will do for sizes up to ½in or 13mm AF, and ½in for anything above that.

Other basic tools you will require include a decent quality set of screwdrivers (flat and crosspoint in a range of sizes), a set of feeler gauges (either imperial or metric), pliers (square nose and needle nose) and that most useful of Land Rover tools, a 2.5lb club hammer. For electrical work you will need wire-cutters, a wire-stripping tool, a decent quality connector crimping tool and a multimeter. There are other tools that you will need for specific tasks and these will be referred to later.

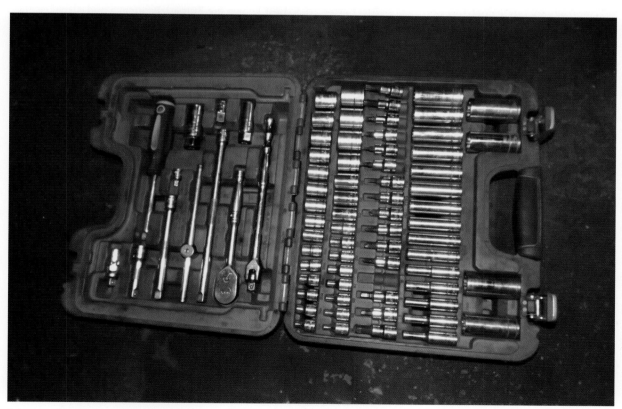

A decent socket set is a must-have item.

More specialized tools – bearing separator and steering box drop arm puller. It may be worth asking a garage to do the job, rather than buying an expensive tool that you may only use once.

Cheap tools are usually cheap for a reason. Spanners and sockets should always be made from chrome-vanadium steel. The 'budget' carbon steel versions have a nasty habit of shattering under load. Good-quality second-hand tools can often be acquired at autojumbles and even car boot sales: look for well-known British or German brands such as Britool, Elora or King Dick. A thirty-year-old set of professional-quality sockets, if not badly worn, will give far better service than a cheap set in a shiny new box.

BUYING PARTS

Parts availability for Series II, IIA and III Land Rovers is in general excellent. There are a few exceptions: some dashboard and trim parts are now very hard to obtain, as are some mechanical parts fitted only to very early production Series IIs. Parts for the early 2-litre engines (petrol and diesel) and the 2.6-litre 'six' are in very short supply. But in most cases a part from a later model can easily be adapted where the original is no longer available.

There are three main types of part:

◆ Genuine parts – supplied by Land Rover dealers in Land Rover packaging, and made to the exact same specification as that fitted to the vehicle when new. The range of parts still available for Series vehicles through the Land Rover dealer network is steadily diminishing, but still worth trying for some of the more obscure items, although at a cost.
◆ Original Equipment Manufacturer (OEM) – made by a company that supplies parts to manufacturers of new vehicles (although not necessarily to Land Rover themselves). These parts are almost always of equivalent quality to the original parts, although their design

and construction may differ. For example, Delphi makes replacement brake cylinders for Land Rovers, but with a steel rather than cast alloy body.
◆ Replacement or 'pattern' – these come from a variety of sources including the Far East, India and Turkey, and are usually sold as 'own brand' parts by one of the major aftermarket Land Rover parts suppliers, of which the best-known are Britpart, Bearmach and Allmakes. They are almost always much cheaper than OEM parts but the quality is unpredictable. Some pattern parts are as good as the originals; others are appalling and even dangerous. For safety-critical parts, genuine or OEM would usually be the preferred choice, but in some cases a pattern part will be the only one available.

Parts are available from a wide variety of outlets – Land Rover main dealers, independent specialists and mail-order retailers, which generally offer next-day delivery and very keen prices. The important thing to remember, particularly when buying mail order, is that if a part is not described as genuine or OEM, it is almost certainly a pattern part.

MANUALS, HANDBOOKS AND PARTS CATALOGUES

For major mechanical work beyond the scope of this book, a comprehensive workshop manual is a must. Undoubtedly, the best manual is that produced by Land Rover for its own dealer network. Manuals for each model are readily available either as new reprints or second-hand. Land Rover also published comprehensive parts catalogues, including exploded diagrams, for every vehicle the company ever made. Like the manuals, these are easily obtained new or second-hand, and are an invaluable source of information when used in conjunction with a workshop manual.

Parts books contain exploded diagrams for every sub-assembly on the vehicle.

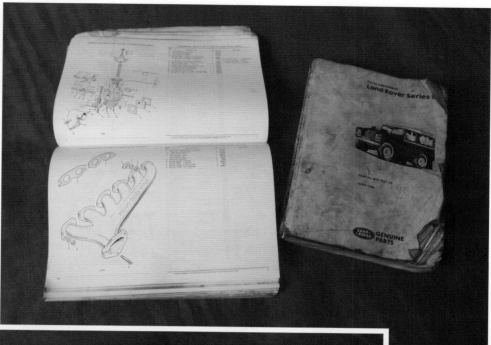

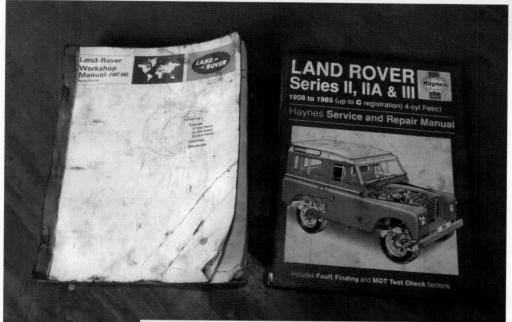

The factory workshop manual is more comprehensive than the Haynes manual, but the latter may be easier for the novice mechanic to follow.

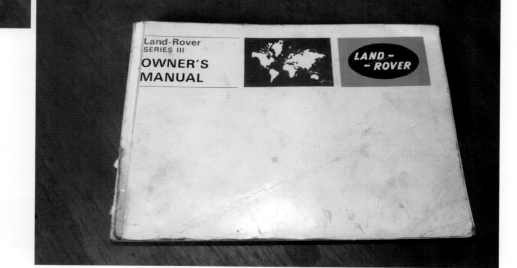

Owner's manuals very seldom come with the vehicle, but can easily be purchased separately.

It is unlikely that your thirty- or forty-year-old Land Rover will come to you with the original owner's handbook. This is less useful than a workshop manual but a nice thing to have, and easily obtained second-hand.

WHEN THINGS GO WRONG

Some of these vehicles are getting on for sixty years old, and when working on components that have never been disturbed, you may run into problems that the workshop manual does not mention. Seized bolts that snap or round off their heads; screws with rusted or worn slots; corroded aluminium castings; cracked iron components; stripped threads – work on old Land Rovers for any length of time and you will come across all of these. But do not panic: there are tools and techniques to deal with any problem you are likely to encounter.

Seized bolts first: there are two kinds to consider: first, a bolt with a nut on the end; second, a bolt that attaches one part of the vehicle to another via a blind threaded hole. Bolts with nuts are usually quite easy to deal with, provided they are reasonably accessible. The most useful techniques are:

◆ Douse the fastener with dismantling fluid (Plus Gas or similar) and wait a few minutes for it to soak in.
◆ If there is a threaded portion protruding beyond the nut, lop it off flush with the nut using a disc cutter before trying to undo it.
◆ If access is good, simply cut off the fastener with a disc cutter, making sure that you do not cut into whatever part of the vehicle it is attached to.

◆ Tighten it up until it shears. This works very well with small fasteners (up to 6mm or ¼in diameter) and is especially useful for the bolts holding the seat box and sills to the side frames.
◆ Drill out the bolt head: this is often the only way you will shift the bolts that hold the seat-belt lower brackets to the side rails. Use a sharp drill bit just a fraction larger than the diameter of the bolt itself, and make sure your hole is perfectly central in the head.

Bolts seized into a blind hole are much trickier. The ones that are most likely to give you problems are the thermostat housing and water pump bolts on the 4-cylinder engines. The first point is that if the bolt does not start to unscrew with moderate force, do not keep levering on it until it snaps. A little patience at this point will save you a lot of time later. An impact gun (either air-operated or cordless) will quite often shock a lightly seized bolt free, and is less likely to shear it off than applying continuous torque with a socket or spanner. You can try very carefully tightening the bolt a fraction, then loosening it, tightening again, and so on until it starts to move. Once you have a very small amount of movement, douse the whole area in Plus Gas and keep working away at it. It can take an hour or more to free off a bolt like this, but drilling out a long broken bolt and reinstating the thread will take much longer. Heating the area around the bolt can help, but you will need quite a lot of heat. A DIY butane blowtorch, as used by plumbers, is unlikely to generate enough heat to make any difference, and a full-sized oxy-acetylene kit is too costly to make any sense for the home-mechanic.

Two broken bolts in this thermostat housing – not looking good.

When things go wrong: Irwin Bolt-Grips, Easy-Out extractors and a comprehensive tap and die set.

If the worst happens and the bolt snaps, all is not necessarily lost. If it has sheared close to the head and you are able to remove the component that it retains, you may find there is enough of the bolt protruding to be able to weld a nut to it. The heat from the welding process will itself help to free the bolt. If the bolt is short, you can try drilling it out, although you will have to be very careful to ensure that you drill straight down the middle of the bolt and not let the drill bit wander off to one side. Start with a small-diameter bit, then use progressively larger sizes. And if the component you are trying to remove is either broken or easily and cheaply replaced, you might consider cutting it off with a disc cutter. You can also try an 'Easy-Out' extractor, which is a bit like a thread tap but with a reverse pitch, coarse tapered thread. The idea is that you drill a hole in the centre of the broken bolt and then screw in the extractor anti-clockwise so that it takes the bolt with it. However, these extractors should be used with great care: they are made from very brittle hardened steel, and if you snap off an extractor in the hole, you will not be able to drill it out.

Rounded nuts and bolt heads are a common problem, especially where the fastener has corroded. You can give yourself a reasonable chance of avoiding this problem by using good-quality, close-fitting six-sided sockets, rather than twelve-point 'bi-hex' ones. But if a head is hopelessly rounded, you will need a set of Irwin bolt extractor sockets. These contain an internal tapered spiral flute, which digs into the remains of the bolt head and will shift almost any bolt, no matter how badly damaged. The smallest sizes can

also be used to grip the protruding end of a broken bolt, as an alternative to welding a nut on the end, but they only work in one direction (anti-clockwise), so cannot be used to work the broken bolt back and forth.

Land Rover did not use many self-tapping screws and the ones you are most likely to encounter are those that hold the floor panels in place. There are two types: large head with a plain slot, and smaller cross-head screws on the front edge of Series III floor panels. The large ones can usually be shifted by giving the head a sharp smack with a

Floor screws, old and new. The correct pattern screws are cheap and readily available from any Land Rover specialist.

hammer, cleaning up the slot with a disc cutter, then using a large, close-fitting screwdriver with a hexagonal shaft and a spanner on the shaft to provide additional leverage. It sometimes helps to tighten the screw a fraction before attempting to lever it. For the crosspoint type, use the disc cutter to cut a slot across the head. And if all else fails, they can be drilled out or the heads cut off.

Stripped or damaged threads are most likely in aluminium castings, but can also result from drilling out broken bolts in iron components. The clutch slave cylinder bolts on the Series III gearbox are particularly prone to stripping their threads. This kind of damage can often be reclaimed using 'Helicoil' or similar thread inserts. The hole is drilled oversize, a new thread cut in it using a thread tap and then a spiral steel insert wound into the hole. This makes for a very strong and durable repair. Thread insert kits are available for almost every thread size you will ever come across, including the BSW threads in Series gearboxes.

Damaged castings: welding up a cracked casting, whether aluminium or cast iron, is a job for a professional. In almost every case it will be quicker and cheaper to find a new or undamaged second-hand replacement. The main exceptions to this are exhaust manifolds on 6-cylinder and V8 models, which are near enough impossible to obtain now. Do not try to weld cast iron yourself: the weld may appear satisfactory but will have almost no penetration or strength.

Leaking radiators: if the hole is small it can usually be repaired by thoroughly cleaning the surrounding area and then smothering it with an epoxy-based repair product (such as Leak-Fix). Make sure the epoxy is pressed well in to the area. Hairline cracks in the top of the radiator are quite common, especially on the older 'wide tank' radiators, and can be repaired in the same way, or by thoroughly cleaning up the area and sealing the crack with solder using a blow-torch. If doing this, you need to be careful not to apply too much heat: the entire radiator is of soldered construction and an excess of heat will melt the solder along the seams.

SERVICING SCHEDULE

The importance of regular servicing for an old Land Rover cannot be overstated. These are simple and robust vehicles, but they were designed in an era where short service intervals were the norm. They contain some very old-fashioned technology and without regular maintenance your Land Rover will let you down, usually at a most inconvenient time. Routine servicing is well within the capabilities of any half-competent home-mechanic and will make a huge difference to your enjoyment and understanding of your vehicle. Over the years Land Rover made various changes to the service schedule, reflecting the upgrading of some mechanical components and the development of better-quality lubricants. The table covers all Series II, IIA and III vehicles subjected to 'typical' usage. For vehicles that are extensively used in arduous off-road conditions and/or in hot, dusty environments, more frequent maintenance may be required.

In the next chapter we will look in more detail at the various procedures listed in the table.

Clutch slave cylinder bolts on the Series III tend to strip their threads.

Servicing schedule

	Weekly	3,000 miles	6,000 miles/ 6 months	12,000 miles/ 1 year	36,000 miles/ 3 years
Underbonnet inspection	X				
Change engine oil and filter (diesel)		X			
Change engine oil and filter (petrol)			X		
Check/reset spark plug gap (petrol)			X		
Check/reset points gap (petrol)			X		
Check ignition timing (petrol)			X		
Adjust idle and mixture (petrol)			X		
Check axle/gearbox fluid levels			X		
Inspect and clean brakes			X		
Inspect steering and suspension			X		
Replace/clean fuel filter				X	
Replace/clean air filter				X	
Replace spark plugs (petrol)				X	
Replace points (petrol)				X	
Adjust valve clearances (except V8)				X	
Replace brake fluid					X
Replace engine coolant					X
Replace axle/gearbox fluids					X

Stripped thread on an exhaust stud: this can be salvaged with a thread insert.

service procedures in detail

RECOMMENDED FLUIDS

Over the years, the recommendations for oil and other fluid specifications have changed as lubricant technology has advanced. However, these vehicles were absolutely not designed to cope with modern lightweight oils, which will leak past the seals.

Fluid specifications		
Application	**Grade**	**Specification**
Petrol engines (all)	15W/40	Mineral or semi-synthetic, API classification SJ or better
Diesel engines	15W/40	Mineral or semi-synthetic, API classification CF or better
Gearbox and transfer box (4- and 6-cylinder), axles, swivel housings, steering box, steering relay	EP90 or EP80W/90	Grade GL4. GL5 should not be used as it is reputed to eat away brass components in some circumstances
Gearbox and transfer box (109 V8, LT95 transmission)	20W/50	Mineral or semi-synthetic. These gearboxes use engine oil: do not fill with EP gear oil as this will break the drive to the oil pump
Brake and clutch master cylinder reservoir	Brake fluid	DOT 4
Cooling system	Antifreeze	Ethylene glycol base, 30% mixture in water for normal conditions, 50% in extremely cold climates
Propshaft and steering grease points	Grease	Standard multipurpose grease

For tired and badly worn engines, 20W/50 oil may help to reduce oil consumption and maintain oil pressure when hot.

Fluid capacities	
	Capacity (ltr)
Engine including filter 2286cc	6.85
Engine including filter 2625cc	7.3
Engine including filter 3528cc	5.7
Gearbox (except 109 V8)	1.5
Gearbox (109 V8)	2.6
Transfer box (except 109 V8)	2.5
Transfer box (109 V8)	3.1
Front axle	1.75
Rear axle (Rover)	1.75
Rear axle (Salisbury)	2.5
Swivel housing (each)	0.5
Cooling system 2286cc	10.2
Cooling system 2625cc	11.2
Cooling system 3528cc	11.3
Overdrive (Fairey)	0.4

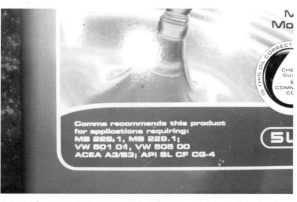

Oil specifications – ACEA and API classifications. This one is SL/CF and will be fine for either petrol or diesel Land Rovers.

UNDERBONNET INSPECTION

This should be done weekly for a vehicle in regular use, before a long journey or when a vehicle has been standing unused for a month or more. With the vehicle standing on a level surface, and the engine not having been started for at least thirty minutes, withdraw the dipstick, wipe it with a clean cloth, re-insert it into the tube ensuring it is pushed fully home, then withdraw it again and inspect the oil-level reading. There will normally be two or three scribed marks. The level should never fall below the lowest of the marks or be topped up above the highest. The difference between the high and low marks is normally around one litre. If the engine oil is low, slowly add fresh oil of the correct type to bring it up to the high mark.

Coolant level next, and this should only be checked with the engine cold. Removing the radiator cap on a hot engine can result in serious scalding. To be absolutely sure of avoiding injury, place a thick cloth over the radiator cap and very slowly open it to allow any pressure to be released gradually. The coolant level should be about an inch (25mm) from the top of the radiator on Series II and earlier IIA models. Later vehicles have a plastic expansion bottle beside the radiator: on these vehicles the radiator should be full of coolant right up to the top of the cap, and the expansion bottle about a third to half full when cold. V8s have a separate expansion tank, which should be around half full: on these vehicles, with the cap removed the tank should be filled about half full, and the bottom radiator hose then squeezed by hand repeatedly to expel air from the top of the radiator and draw in coolant from the expansion tank.

Brake and clutch fluid: most Series II and IIA vehicles have a combined metal reservoir (known affectionately as the 'bean can') for brake and clutch fluid. Series IIIs have separate reservoirs for each. Brake and clutch systems should be topped up with fresh, clean brake fluid from a sealed

container to the maximum mark where visible, and to just below the top of the reservoir where there is no maximum mark. These fluid levels should only fall very slowly and will not normally need topping up between 6,000 mile services: any sudden fall in level indicates a fluid leak in the system, which requires urgent investigation.

Check the fan belt to ensure it is adequately tensioned and not starting to crack or fray. The belt tension should be set so that the belt can be deflected between finger and thumb around an inch (25mm) at the midpoint between water pump and alternator or dynamo without undue effort. To reset the belt tension, loosen the two nuts and bolts holding the dynamo or alternator to its mounting bracket, the bolt holding the slotted adjuster to the engine and, finally, the bolt (or nut and bolt) that secures the slotted adjuster to the dynamo or alternator. Lever the alternator away from the engine using a large screwdriver until the correct tension is achieved, tighten the slotted adjuster bolt, recheck the belt tension and then tighten the remaining bolts.

Finally, carry out a visual inspection of the remaining underbonnet components. You are looking for components that are worn, insecure or in danger of premature failure. Pay particular attention to cooling system hoses and inspect them for signs of cracking or leakage around the ends. Wiring harnesses should all be secure and not rubbing on moving components. Take a quick look underneath the vehicle to ensure that no new oil leaks have

The 'bean can': combined clutch and brake fluid reservoir found on most Series II and IIA vehicles.

Aftermarket twin reservoirs replacing the original 'bean can'.

Series III has separate reservoirs for brake and clutch fluid. The brake reservoir is the larger of the two.

appeared, and ensure that the exhaust system is securely mounted and not about to fall off or disintegrate. Before a long journey it is also wise to check the tyre pressures with a gauge, and to inspect them for cracks, cuts and bulges that may indicate imminent failure.

CHANGE ENGINE OIL AND FILTER

This procedure should be carried out every 3,000 miles for diesel engines and every 6,000 miles for petrol. It should be done with the engine warm and the vehicle standing on a level surface. You will need a large receptacle for the old oil: the capacity on these engines ranges from six to seven litres. Old oil should be disposed of in a responsible manner: local councils normally provide a facility for its safe disposal at their recycling centres.

Standard canister oil filter on the 2.25 engine comes in two lengths: earlier engines had a much longer filter and housing. This is the more common later version.

'Spin-on' oil filter and housing from later vehicles will fit Series engines.

4- and 6-cylinder Engines

With the receptacle placed underneath, loosen and remove the sump drain plug and allow the old oil to drain out. Remove the old copper washer from the drain plug and replace it with a new one. Wipe clean the area around the drain hole in the sump, reinsert the plug and tighten. Now position the receptacle under the oil filter housing, undo the central bolt and carefully remove the filter canister, ensuring that you do not spill oil on the ground. Remove the filter element, drain any remaining oil from the canister and then clean it out using rags or paper towels.

There is a rubber sealing ring around the edge of the filter housing: this needs to be prised out with a small screwdriver, the recess cleaned and a new seal (which will come with the new oil filter) pressed into place ensuring it is correctly located all the way round. Place the new filter in the canister ensuring it is centrally located on the spring-loaded plate inside the canister, offer the canister up to the filter housing ensuring that the upper end of the filter locates centrally on the protruding lugs in the centre of the housing and engage the bolt. Carefully tighten the bolt, ensuring that the upper edge of the canister sits squarely in the recess in the filter housing. Fill the engine with 6 litres of fresh oil, start it and ensure the oil pressure light extinguishes, then switch off and leave for at least ten minutes. Finally, check the oil level and top up as necessary.

V8 Engines

These have a high-mounted oil pump, which is prone to air locks if allowed to drain. The recommended procedure for these engines is to drain and refill the sump first, run the engine and only then change the oil filter. The sump should be left empty for as little time as possible: as soon as the flow of old oil from the drain plug slows to a trickle, refit the plug and immediately pour in 5 litres of fresh oil. Then start the engine and ensure the oil light goes out. After this, the oil filter can be removed (it is a 'spin-on' type and will normally require a strap-type filter wrench to loosen), and a new filter fitted and tightened by hand. Before removing the old filter it is a good idea to prime the new one by trickling in fresh oil until it is about three-quarters full: this will minimize the period of oil starvation on startup. With the new filter fitted, restart the engine, again check that the oil light extinguishes, then switch off, check and top up.

Spin-On Filter Conversions

These are a fairly popular modification for 4-cylinder engines and make filter changes a little less fiddly. The complete filter head from a 2.5 petrol or non-turbo diesel engine (Ninety/One Ten 1984–90) will bolt straight on in place of the old canister assembly, using the original mounting bolts and a new gasket. Alternatively, new conversion kits are available from a couple of specialist suppliers.

PLUGS AND POINTS (PETROL ENGINES)

These engines use old-fashioned contact breaker (or 'points') ignition systems, which work very well when in good order but depend on the correct gap settings for plugs and points in order to generate a good, healthy spark. Over time the plug gap will increase as the electrodes erode, and the points' gap will close up as the plastic lobe on the points wears. Both settings should be checked every six months using a feeler gauge. Plugs should be removed one at a time using the correct deep-sided plug socket, the gap checked and adjusted, if necessary, using a pair of needle-nose pliers to bend the outer electrode. On refitting, plugs should be screwed in finger-tight, then tightened a quarter-turn. Great care should be taken not

Inside a Lucas 25D distributor.

to cross-thread the plugs, especially on 6-cylinder and V8 engines, which have soft, aluminium cylinder heads.

To set the points gap, first remove the distributor cap (two spring clips) and then pull the rotor arm off the end of the shaft. On 4-cylinder engines, access is much easier if the air cleaner and intake hose are removed first. The engine should then be slowly turned by hand until the points are fully open. The engine can usually be turned by grasping the cooling fan or by use of the starting handle (if the vehicle still has one). With the points fully open, the gap can be checked and adjusted, if required. On most distributors this is achieved by loosening the slotted screw retaining the points to the distributor, moving the points' assembly and tightening the screw. V8 engines have a small hexagon-headed adjuster screw protruding from the distributor body towards the front. If the points are badly burned or pitted, they should be replaced along with the condenser.

Before replacing the rotor arm, put a couple of drops of machine oil into the centre of the distributor shaft and give the outside of the shaft a thin smear of Vaseline where the points' lobe bears on it. Some distributors are fitted with felt pads to lubricate this area: these should be lubricated with machine oil until wet but not dripping. Finally, the rotor arm should be inspected for signs of cracks, 'tracking' (where electricity is conducted across the insulation leaving a visible line) or excess burning at the metal contact. The distributor cap should also be inspected for 'tracking' and the spring-loaded carbon brush inside checked to ensure it is undamaged and can move freely.

CHECK IGNITION TIMING

It is important that the ignition system should generate a spark at exactly the right point in the combustion cycle, just before the piston reaches the top of its travel on the compression stroke. Too early and combustion will take place before the piston goes over top dead centre, which can lead to piston damage; too late and much of the energy created by combustion is simply wasted, resulting in lack of power and overheating. The correct timing varies according to engine specification and the type of distributor fitted. There are three ways to set it:

◆ **Static timing.** With the engine stationary and the timing marks lined up, the distributor is slowly rotated until the points are just beginning to open. This provides a rough starting point but does not take accurate account of any wear in the distributor shaft and drive gear.
◆ **Dynamic timing.** This uses a stroboscopic timing light shone onto the timing marks with the engine running: the distributor is then slowly turned until the marks line up.
◆ **Road test.** Having set up the static timing, the vehicle is then road tested, the timing advanced a couple of degrees, road tested again and so on until it can be heard 'pinking' (a light tinkling sound) under load. At this point the timing will be slightly too far advanced, so it is retarded a couple of degrees. This method is the most time-consuming but achieves the optimum timing setting for that particular engine and distributor.

Timing pointer and notch on the front crankshaft pulley (later petrol engines).

Timing pointer and scribed marks inside the flywheel housing (earlier petrols and diesels).

The first stage is to identify the correct timing marks for either static or dynamic timing, by reference to the workshop manual. On engines made up to around 1967, the timing marks are on the edge of the flywheel, accessed via a small window on the upper side of the flywheel housing and very hard to access and read, especially with the engine running. Later engines have a pointer attached to the front of the timing cover and a notch on the crankshaft pulley. Some engines have a serrated pointer and a single notch; others have a single pointer and multiple notches. It is helpful to highlight the correct pointer and notch combination with Tippex, especially when using a stroboscope to set the timing dynamically.

To adjust the timing, older Lucas distributors have a knurled wheel on the side marked 'A R'. This can be turned to advance or retard the timing by a small amount, assuming that the mechanism is not seized solid (as it often is). There is a clamp ring at the base of the distributor (clamping plate and nut on V8s) that can be loosened just enough to allow the distributor body to be turned by hand, but not so loose that it will move by itself with the engine running. When adjusting the timing with the engine running, be very careful not to come into contact with any of the plug leads, as this can give you a nasty jolt. It may be safer (especially if you have a heart pacemaker) to switch off the engine before attempting to move the distributor. It goes without saying that when working on a running engine you should be very careful to keep clothing, body parts and the timing light well away from the fan blades.

ADJUST IDLE AND MIXTURE SETTINGS

4-cylinder engines may be fitted with any one of several different carburettors. Vehicles up to 1967 used the Solex PA40; 1967 onwards, the Zenith 36IV; and both types are often replaced with the aftermarket Weber 34ICH. All three are fixed-jet carburettors with idle speed and mixture controlled via external adjustment screws. 6-cylinder engines usually have a single Stromberg carburettor with mixture adjustment via an external knurled screw or (on later models) a movable needle adjusted with a special tool inserted into the top of the carburettor. V8s normally

have twin Strombergs with the movable needle system, but some may have been retro-fitted with SU carburettors, which usually have external mixture adjusting screws.

Adjusting 4-cylinder engines is relatively easy. Having first set up the ignition timing, and with the engine warm, adjust the idle screw to achieve the desired idle speed. These engines idle more slowly than a modern engine: too high an idle speed can lead to the engine 'running on' for a few seconds when switched off. Ideally, the idle speed should be set as low as the engine will tolerate while still running smoothly. The mixture screw is then turned slowly clockwise until the engine starts to falter, then anti-clockwise as far as is needed to restore a smooth idle. If the engine starts to run hesitantly as soon as the mixture screw is turned, it is probably already adjusted too far clockwise and should be turned anti-clockwise until the engine runs smoothly. This may result in the engine speed increasing, in which case the idle screw should be adjusted to bring the speed down again and the mixture readjusted. If you have access to an exhaust gas analyser, this can be used to check your work but, provided the carburettor is in reasonable order, the above procedure should bring CO emissions well within acceptable levels.

For the 6-cylinder engine, first remove the air intake from the carburettor, then set the idle speed (external screw adjuster similar to the 4-cylinder versions). Using a very fine screwdriver, carefully lift up the dashpot inside the air intake about $\frac{1}{16}$in (1.5mm) and observe the result. If the engine stumbles, the mixture is too weak. If the speed rises significantly, it is too rich. If it rises very slightly and stabilizes, the mixture setting is near enough spot-on. On older Strombergs with an external mixture control, the setting is easily adjusted. Later versions require the dashpot plunger (black knurled object on top of the carburettor) to be removed and a special two-part tool inserted into the hole. The outer part is engaged with the dashpot and held stationary, while the inner part locates on the end of the jet needle and is turned to raise or lower the needle and adjust the mixture accordingly.

Setting up the carburettors on V8 engines is more complicated, as there are two of them. They need to be balanced so that both are admitting the same amount of air

Pump dispenser is the best way to fill gearboxes and axles with oil.

at idle. An experienced mechanic can do this by ear, but for the novice it will be easier to use a carburettor balancing tool. While doing this, the linkage between the two carburettors should be loosened so that the two can be adjusted independently of each other. Once the carburettors are balanced and the correct idle speed achieved, the mixture for each carburettor can be set using the same procedure as for the 6-cylinder Stromberg. When the balance, idle and mixture are all correct, the clamp bolts for the linkage between the two carburettors can be tightened. V8s tend to be rather marginal on exhaust emissions for MoT purposes, and should really be checked using an exhaust gas analyser, as they often run best when producing CO emissions well above acceptable limits.

On all carburettor types, the linkages should be checked for wear and lubricated at all moving points (of which there are many). Get an assistant to depress the accelerator pedal fully (with the engine off) and check that this translates into full movement of the throttle arm on the carburettor. Check also that the throttle arm closes fully when the pedal is released, without needing a poke from your finger. On 4-cylinder vehicles there is a spring-loaded bellcrank attached to the nearside bulkhead support bracket. If the throttle arm does not return easily by itself, the spring tension can be increased by slackening the securing nut on the bellcrank and rotating the hexagonal body against the direction of throttle arm travel.

CHECK AXLE AND GEARBOX FLUID LEVELS

The gearbox, transfer box, axles, swivel housings and steering box are all prone to leak oil and should be checked every 6,000 miles (or more frequently if they leak really badly). The procedure for checking levels is basically the same for all these items: locate the fill/level plug, place a drip tray underneath it, remove the plug and add the correct type of oil until it starts to trickle out, then refit the plug. A pump-type dispenser is invaluable for this purpose. Fill/level plug locations are as follows:

◆ **Front axle** – on the front face of the axle casing, about halfway up. Normally $^{9}/_{16}$in square, male head.
◆ **Rear axle** – either on the rear face of the axle casing or on the side of the differential. Filler on rear face may be $^{9}/_{16}$in male, square head or $^{1}/_{2}$in square, female. Differential mounted filler is six-sided and usually $^{3}/_{4}$in.
◆ **Swivel housings** – on the rear face of the housing, about halfway up; $^{1}/_{2}$in square, male head.
◆ **Gearbox** – on the left-hand side of the gearbox casing. Normally $^{1}/_{2}$in square, male head, some early gearboxes have a much smaller ($^{7}/_{16}$in square head) level plug and a top-mounted filler secured by a spring clip and accessed by a removable plate on the transmission tunnel. The LT95 gearbox on the 109 V8 has a six-sided brass plug and sealing washer instead.

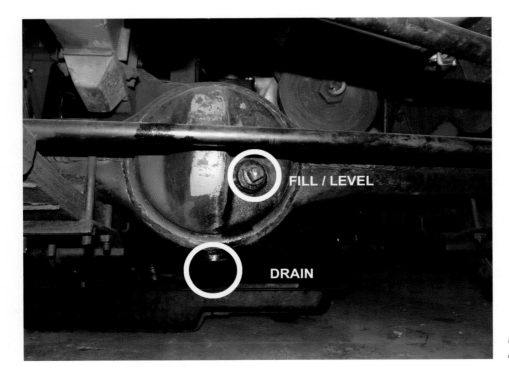

Front axle fill/level and drain plugs.

Rover rear axle fill/level plug.

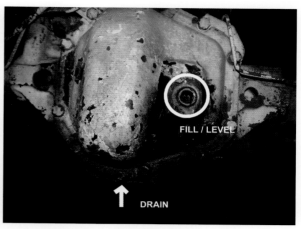

Salisbury rear axle fill/level and drain plugs.

Swivel housing fill/level plug.

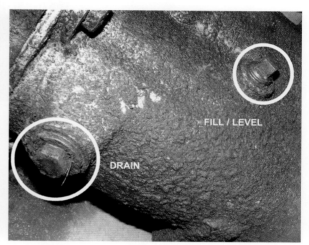

Main gearbox fill/level and drain plugs.

Top mounted oil filler on a military gearbox.

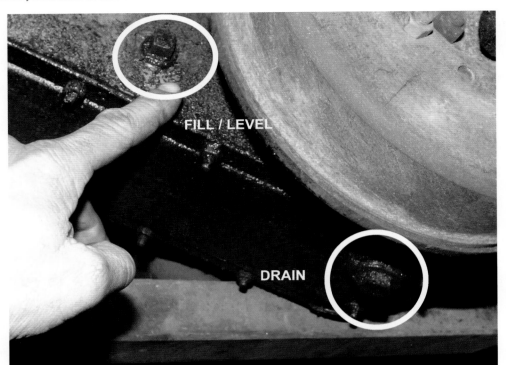

Transfer box fill/level and drain plugs.

FILL / LEVEL

DRAIN

Hexagonal plug on the transfer box is not an oil filler and should be left alone, as there is a strong spring underneath it.

Impact driver for removing brake drum screws.

◆ **Transfer box** – on the rear face of the casing. Normally ½in square, male head; some early transfer boxes have the smaller ⁷⁄₁₆in plug and a larger brass six-sided filler plug on top of the transfer box casing near the transmission brake.

◆ **Steering box** – on the top face of the casing; ⁷⁄₁₆in square, male head.

◆ **Overdrive** – on the top of the casing; ¹³⁄₁₆in hexagonal plug incorporating dipstick. The oil level should just reach the end of the dipstick.

INSPECT AND CLEAN BRAKES

This aspect of servicing is often neglected until the brakes actually stop working altogether, as it requires the wheels and brake drums to be removed. Jack up the vehicle and support on axle stands, then remove the wheels. The brake drums are secured to the hubs with either one or three countersunk screws for which you will need an impact

Using a bolt screwed into the extractor hole to remove the brake drum.

Peel back the dust covers on the wheel cylinders to check for leaks. This one is nice and dry.

driver. Then slacken off the brake adjusters (assuming they are not seized solid) so that the drum rotates freely. There is a threaded hole in the face of the drum to aid removal: the size is ⅜in BSW. If you can obtain a bolt of this size, it will greatly aid removal of the drums, which are often rusted to the hub. Failing this, try striking the front face of the drum with a club hammer to shock it free. Never hit the edge of the drum from behind as it is very fragile and will shatter and possibly send sharp splinters into your eye. In extreme cases, where a drum has not been removed for many years, it may be necessary to remove the complete hub assembly and then separate the hub and drum with a press.

Once the drum has been removed, the internal components can be inspected. The hub should present a dry

appearance. If wet, this may be due to a failed hub seal or fluid leaking from the wheel cylinder. Peel back the rubber cover(s) on each wheel cylinder: the inside should be dry. If it is wet with fluid, the cylinder seals are past their best and the cylinder should usually be changed. Replacement seal kits are available as a cheap but not always satisfactory fix. Using a large screwdriver, try to push the end of each piston into the cylinder: a seized piston again means that the cylinder is scrap.

The linings on the brake shoes should have plenty of material left (at least ⅛in/3mm) and not be cracked or contaminated with oil or brake fluid. The shoes should be free to move on their pivot points, with return springs intact and correctly positioned. Brake adjusters should

Brake adjuster on 10in front brakes.

be lubricated and checked to ensure they are not seized. Finally, the brake drums should be checked for excess wear and grooving: they are not expensive and if obviously worn should be replaced as an axle set, along with the brake shoes. Brake drums and shoes in good condition should be lightly abraded with 80 grit sandpaper to remove any dirt, then the drums refitted followed by the drum screws. A smear of copper grease around the joint between the drum and hub, and on the threads of the drum screws, will do no harm at all.

Brakes should be adjusted with the wheels fitted and nuts tightened to clamp the drum securely to the hub. While rotating each wheel in turn by hand in the normal direction of travel, tighten each adjuster (usually clockwise) until the wheel locks. Back it off until the wheel turns freely, tighten it until the brake just starts to bind, then back off one notch. Once all the brakes have been adjusted, pump the brake pedal three or four times, then check that all four wheels still rotate freely. Brake drums are often not per-

fectly round, and a slight drag at one point in the wheel's rotation should not give cause for concern.

Rigid, metal brake pipes should be inspected along their entire length. Steel pipes should be free from anything more than very light surface rust, with no obvious pitting. Brake pipe unions should not be heavily corroded, and all brake pipes should be secured to the chassis and axles at intervals of no more than 45cm (18in). Carefully inspect the flexible hoses, bending them back to look for signs of cracking in the rubber, or 'ballooning' where fluid has got between the inner and outer layers due to failure of the inner layer.

INSPECT STEERING AND SUSPENSION

This is largely a visual inspection and should be carried out while the vehicle is still on axle stands, with wheels fitted but clear of the ground. Wheel bearings first – rotate each wheel by hand. It should rotate smoothly without roughness or rumbling. Grasp each wheel top and bottom, and try to rock it up and down. There should be no discernible movement. If movement is detected in either front wheel, ask an assistant to depress the brake pedal firmly and repeat the test. If movement can still be felt, the most likely cause is excess play or wear in the steering swivel assembly.

This steering arm securing nut and bolt often work loose causing excess steering play.

Leaf springs should be inspected for leaves that are broken or splayed apart due to rust building up between them, and the rubber bushes at each end checked. A bush that has broken up internally should be obvious as the pin that runs through it will no longer be central in the bush. Shock absorbers should be free of oil leaks, and there should be no slack in the bushes at either end.

The steering joints (six in total) are protected by rubber boots, which should be intact and not split or perished. Grasp each steering rod adjacent to the joint and try to move it up and down: there should be no play at all in the joint. A worn joint is dangerous and should be changed. The drop arm attached to the steering relay can work loose on its shaft: again, grasp the arm and check that it cannot be moved by hand. Turn the steering onto full left and right lock and check that the tyres are not rubbing against the springs: lock stops are fitted to the swivel housings and can be adjusted if required. The chrome swivels on the front axle should be free of rust pitting and oil leaks.

While all four wheels are still off the ground, the propeller shafts should be checked. Grasp each end (with the handbrake off) and try to waggle it from side

Grease nipples on propshaft joints require regular attention.

to side – any movement in the joint should be obvious. There is a grease nipple on each joint and another one on the shaft close to the sliding spline: all of these should be greased using a grease gun. Finally, before lowering the vehicle to the ground, the transmission brake should be adjusted. There is a square-headed adjuster on the back-plate: turn this while rotating the brake drum by hand until the drum starts to drag, then back it off a quarter of a turn. Operate the handbrake lever: the handbrake should engage fully within four or five clicks of the ratchet. If this cannot be achieved through adjustment, either the hand-brake shoes are worn out, or the mechanism itself is worn or defective.

REPLACE/CLEAN FUEL FILTER

Most 4-cylinder petrol engines have a simple gauze strainer inside the fuel pump. 6-cylinder and V8 engines have a paper element filter inside a small metal canister in the engine bay. Diesel engines have a much larger metal-cased filter attached to the bulkhead. When working on petrol engines, make sure all potential sources of ignition are kept away, as some petrol will inevitably be spilt. Mop up spilt petrol immediately and dispose of safely.

◆ **4-cylinder petrol.** Place a drip tray under the fuel pump, unscrew the thumbwheel securing the glass sediment bowl to the pump, remove the sediment bowl, empty it and clean it thoroughly. Remove the rubber seal and gauze strainer from the pump, clean the strainer and check the seal: replace if hardened or damaged. Refit the strainer, seal and bowl and tighten the thumbwheel. Start engine and check for leaks.

◆ **6-cylinder and V8 petrol.** Place a drip tray under the filter assembly, remove the central ⁷⁄₁₆in bolt and detach the metal canister from the filter head. Remove and discard the paper element, thoroughly clean the canister and insert a new element. Carefully prise the two rubber seals from the filter head and fit the new ones supplied with the filter, along with the rubber O-ring under the securing bolt washer. Refit the canister and tighten the bolt slowly, ensuring that the edge of the canister is correctly engaged with the groove in the filter head. Start the engine and check for leaks.

◆ **Diesel engines.** Place a drip tray under the filter assembly, then loosen the central ⁷⁄₁₆in bolt while supporting the filter and bottom bowl from underneath. Remove the filter and bowl (trying not to spill too much diesel in the process), discard the filter and clean the bowl. Replace the rubber seals in the filter head and the O-ring on the bolt as per the previous section, locate the lower rubber seal in the bowl followed by the filter, push the filter and bowl into place on the filter head and tighten the securing bolt.

The diesel fuel system now needs to be bled. First, crack open the ⅝in banjo bolt on top of the fuel filter housing, then operate the priming lever on the fuel pump until fuel emerges from the banjo free from air bubbles. Tighten the banjo bolt. There are two ⁵⁄₁₆in bleed screws on the injec-

Oil-bath air-filter split into its two parts. The bowl should be cleaned and filled with engine oil up to the 'Max' mark.

tion pump: crack open each in turn (the lower one first) and again operate the priming lever until no more air bubbles emerge, then tighten the bleed screw. Ensure when doing this that the engine stop lever is in the 'run' position: on a Series III with the interlocking stop cable and ignition switch, the ignition key will have to be turned to the 'on' position to release the stop cable. Start the engine and hold it at medium speed for 30 seconds to purge any remaining air. If the engine dies, repeat the bleeding process. And if after bleeding it a second time the engine will not restart, crack open the unions on all four injectors, then crank the engine on the starter until fuel emerges from the unions. Then tighten the unions and the engine should now start.

REPLACE/CLEAN AIR FILTER

4- and 6-cylinder models have an old-fashioned oil-bath air-filter, which will need periodic cleaning. The filter is split into two parts held together by spring clips. The bottom half contains oil: this should be emptied out and disposed of as for used engine oil, the bowl thoroughly cleaned to remove any sludge and then refilled to the level indicated on the inside with clean engine oil. The mesh filter should be separated from the upper half, cleaned in paraffin or kerosene, and allowed to dry before the filter is reassembled and refitted. The 109 V8 has replacement paper element air-filters: these can be accessed by removing the cast aluminium U-shaped air-intake pipes, followed by the air-filter end covers, which are secured with spring clips. The filters are retained to the end covers with wing nuts and plates.

REPLACE SPARK PLUGS AND POINTS

The procedure for replacing spark plugs is the same as for removing and re-gapping them. Do not assume that the new plugs are supplied with the gap correctly set: always check each one before fitting. 4-cylinder engines have two different types of plug depending on whether they are 7:1 or 8:1 compression ratio. To identify which type of engine you have, refer to Chapter 8. The points set will be secured to the distributor baseplate with a screw. On the Ducellier distributor, the assembly is in two parts, with the fixed contact secured with a screw and the moving contact

New plugs, points and condenser are normally all you will need to get your engine running sweetly.

with a hairpin-shaped clip, which is very easy to lose. The condenser is secured with a single screw in all cases. When replacing points on the older Lucas distributor, note that the wires have large, ring terminals on the end and locate over a plastic 'top hat' insulator. The terminals must be

located centrally on this insulator to ensure that they do not touch the metal pivot post, otherwise the vehicle will not start. Before refitting the distributor cap, ensure that the wires inside the distributor are routed clear of the points and distributor body. Whenever the points are replaced, the points' gap and ignition timing must be reset.

ADJUST VALVE CLEARANCES

To maintain optimum engine performance, valve clearances should be checked every 12,000 miles, except for the V8 engine, which has hydraulic tappets that require no adjustment. On 4- and 6-cylinder engines, the valve clearances are measured with a feeler gauge and adjusted with a screw and locking nut. The first stage is to remove the rocker cover, and also the side cover plate on 6-cylinder engines. The cork gaskets that seal these should be discarded and new ones fitted on reassembly, otherwise the engine will leak oil everywhere.

On the 4-cylinder engine, the procedure for adjustment is very simple with the valves easily accessible. The basic principle is that each valve should be adjusted when the lobe on the camshaft is directly opposite the valve. It is impossible to see the camshaft itself, but the design of these engines is such that when one valve is fully open, another will be fully closed. The workshop manual gives the order in which to check the valves, but this will not be needed if you can grasp the 'rule of nine' principle. Valves are numbered one to eight, with one being at the front of the engine. If you add the number of the valve that is fully open to the number of the valve to be checked, the total will be nine.

WHICH DISTRIBUTOR DO YOU HAVE?

4-cylinder petrol engines may have one of three different types of distributor. The most common is the Lucas 22D/25D: this has a domed, black cap and knurled wheel on the side marked 'A R'. The Lucas 45D has a flatter top to the cap and lacks the knurled wheel. The Ducellier usually has a brown distributor cap, with the condenser mounted on the outside of the body and secured with a metal clamp and screw. The three types are interchangeable. 6- and 8-cylinder engines were only ever supplied with one type of distributor.

Ducellier distributor: note brown cap and cylindrical condenser mounted on side of body.

Main part numbers for ignition components

	Lucas 22/25D	Lucas 45D	Ducellier	6-cylinder	V8
Points	RTC3270	RTC3282	RTC3283	RTC3270	608158
Condenser	RTC3472	RTC3474	RTC3473	RTC3472	RTC3472
Rotor arm	RTC3612	RTC3614	RTC3616	RTC4542	RTC3613
Cap	566859	RTC3278	RTC3295	605544	605190

Checking valve clearances using a feeler gauge.

So you need to turn the engine (using the starting handle or a large spanner on the crankshaft pulley bolt) while watching the valves. When one valve is fully open, subtract the number of that valve from nine and you have the number of the valve to be checked. For example, when number four valve is open you should check number five (9 – 4 = 5), with number seven valve open you check number two and so on. 6-cylinder engines use the 'rule of thirteen' but are a little trickier as the exhaust valves are located in the engine block and accessible (with difficulty) via a cover plate on the side. The exhaust valves are numbered oddly from one to eleven, inlet valves (on top of the head) evenly from two to twelve.

To check the valve clearances, select the appropriate thickness of feeler gauge and slide it between the end of the valve stem and the tip of the rocker on the valve to be checked. Then loosen the locknut, tighten the adjuster screw until the feeler gauge just starts to be pinched, then slacken it just enough for the gauge to slide freely. Hold the screw stationary and tighten the nut. On petrol engines, if you find that the clearance on the exhaust valves has tightened up, this is a sign that the valves are starting to recess into the head, normally caused by use of unleaded petrol without an additive.

REPLACE BRAKE FLUID

Brake fluid is 'hygroscopic', which is to say that it absorbs moisture from the atmosphere over time. This cannot be

seen, but gradually lowers the boiling point of the fluid until it can boil when the brakes get hot (for example, descending a long, steep hill). This will result in complete brake failure and it is therefore a very good idea to drain and refill the braking system every three years. The vehicle should be placed on axle stands and the wheels removed. There is a bleed nipple on the back of each brake cylinder: the first step is to check that all of these can be opened and are free of debris. Attach a length of clear tubing to each nipple in turn, place the other end in a receptacle, and attempt to open the nipple (anti-clockwise), ideally with a six-sided ring spanner. Bleed nipples are usually 10mm or 7⁄16in. If the nipple is seized solid, the corners are rounded

Vacuum brake bleeder powered by compressed air.

off or it shears when you try to undo it, it will usually be easier to replace the affected wheel cylinder than to try and extract the remains of the nipple. If the nipple opens but no fluid comes out, it is blocked and will need to be removed and cleaned out or replaced with a new one.

Once you have established that the brakes can actually be bled, slacken each nipple in turn and pump the brake pedal until only air emerges. Now refill the brake reservoir with fresh, clean fluid from a sealed container, and pump the brake pedal three or four times to draw fluid into the master cylinder. The brakes can now be bled. There are several ways to do this. The traditional method involves two people: one to operate the brake pedal, the other to open and close each bleed nipple. The person operating the nipple has control of the operation. He opens the nipple and says 'Down', at which point the person in the cab slowly depresses the brake pedal, taking about two seconds to reach the floor. When the pedal reaches the floor, the pedal operator repeats 'Down', the nipple operator closes the nipple and says 'Up'. The pedal operator now slowly releases the pedal, taking about a second to return to the top of its travel, at which point he repeats 'Up'. This procedure is repeated at each wheel cylinder, starting from the one furthest from the master cylinder, until fluid free from air bubbles emerges from all four nipples. Each cylinder may have to be bled two or three times to achieve this. The fluid level in the master cylinder should be repeatedly checked throughout the operation: it takes about ten pumps to empty it, and if air is drawn into the master cylinder, the whole process will have to be started again.

Several different 'one-man' brake bleeders are available to remove the need for an assistant. The simplest type consists of a tube with a one-way valve that is attached to the nipple and the other end placed in a jar of clean brake fluid.

The nipple is opened and the pedal pumped until no air can be heard bubbling into the fluid. (This does not work well in a noisy workshop.) Pressure bleeders (such as the Gunson Eezibleed) have a reservoir bottle, a tight-fitting cap, which screws onto the fluid reservoir, and an airline that is attached to a tyre to pressurize the entire braking system. Each nipple can be opened in turn until fluid clear from bubbles emerges. This is delightfully simple but it can be difficult to get a good seal at the reservoir, with the risk of blowing brake fluid everywhere under pressure. Note that brake fluid is a very effective paint stripper and should be washed off immediately it comes into contact with any painted surface. The final type of bleeder is the vacuum type, either using a hand pump or an air compressor to operate it. This is again easy to operate, but tends to draw air past the threads on the bleed nipple, making it hard to tell whether all the air has been drawn out of the braking system.

Vehicles fitted with twin-cylinder 11in front brakes (all 109s and post-1980 88s) can be notoriously difficult to bleed, as the design tends to trap air behind the pistons. If you are unable to bleed the air out using conventional methods, you will need to remove the brake drum and shoes, then clamp both pistons firmly into the cylinders with 'G' clamps. The brakes can then be bled using your preferred method. When removing the clamps, release them slowly so that the pistons do not spring outwards and draw in air past the seals. The shoes and drum can then be refitted and the treatment repeated for the other side.

REPLACE ENGINE COOLANT

Antifreeze performs two separate functions. First, it lowers the freezing point of the coolant, providing frost protection in cold weather. Second, it contains corrosion inhibitors to protect the internals of the cooling system. This is particularly important on V8 engines, where plain water can rapidly eat away at the water passages inside the engine. The corrosion inhibitors degrade with age, so the coolant should be replaced every three years, regardless of mileage.

The first stage is to drain the radiator. Most vehicles (except V8s) have a drain tap or plug located on the bottom of the radiator. If this is not present, the bottom hose will have to be removed. The escaping coolant should be drained into a bucket (as far as possible) and disposed of safely. Antifreeze has a taste that cats and dogs find very attractive, and it will kill them even in fairly small quantities. The engine block should now be drained. 4-cylinder engines have a drain plug or tap on the left side of the engine block beneath the manifold and about halfway down the side of the block. V8s have two square-headed drain plugs, one each side of the block underneath the exhaust manifolds.

If the coolant that emerges is rusty in colour, the cooling system should be flushed through, either using a garden hose or by filling it with one of the coolant flushing solutions available from car accessory shops. Once the system is clean, it can then be slowly refilled with an appropriate mixture of ethylene glycol antifreeze and water. Around 30 per cent antifreeze should give adequate winter protection for most European countries. The cooling system capacity of these vehicles is quite large – around two gallons or nine litres in all. V8 engines are particularly prone to air locking when refilling. They should be filled via the removable plug on top of the radiator, rather than the cap on the reservoir, and it helps to detach one of the hoses at the heater to release air trapped in the engine block.

REPLACE AXLE AND GEARBOX FLUIDS

Land Rover's recommendation is that this is done every two years or 24,000 miles, but unless the vehicle is regularly used

Plain water and rust flakes indicate the need to flush the cooling system.

in arduous off-road conditions, this can safely be stretched to 36,000 miles with modern oils. There are drain plugs at the bottom of each axle, the gearbox and transfer box, which are sealed with copper washers (apart from Salisbury rear axles and some very late Series IIIs with ½in square, female taper drain plugs), which should be replaced on refitting. The filling procedure has already been described. When draining the gearbox oil it is not unusual to find fragments of metal inside the hollow drain plug: these are most likely to be from the synchromesh mechanism and do not usually indicate impending catastrophe, although gear selection will become progressively more 'crunchy'.

The front swivel housings have very small hexagonal-headed drain plugs and are very slow to drain. This operation should ideally be carried out after a long run to warm and thin the oil inside. Swivel housings that have been filled with semi-fluid grease (*see* Chapter 10) do not need to be drained and refilled, nor should they need topping up. A swivel assembly that is badly worn enough to leak when filled with semi-fluid grease is well overdue for rebuilding.

brakes, steering and suspension

Carrying out routine servicing work will give you the confidence to tackle more difficult and complicated repairs to your Land Rover. This and the following four chapters are not intended as a comprehensive guide, but rather to be read in conjunction with a good workshop manual. The idea is to highlight some of the problems you may face when working on a vehicle that is getting on for half a century old, and which are not always adequately covered in the manual.

It should go without saying that brakes, suspension and steering are safety-critical systems. Defective workmanship in these areas has the potential to kill you, your passengers and other road users. A few years ago a Land Rover left the road and landed upside-down in a river. The driver survived but his two children were killed. The accident was found to have been caused by dangerously inadequate repairs to the braking system, which had been carried out by the driver. This should be a stark warning to anyone contemplating home maintenance. Having said that, the braking, steering and suspension systems on these vehicles are simple and robust, and a little common sense will go a long way.

REPLACING BRAKE SHOES AND DRUMS

Shoes and drums should always be replaced as an axle set. With the drums removed (as described in Chapter 6),

replacement is relatively easy. There are three different types of brake:

◆ Ten-inch single leading shoe (10in SLS) – rear axle on all 88in vehicles, front axle on 88in up to 1980.
◆ Eleven-inch single leading shoe (11in SLS) – rear axle on 109in vehicles.
◆ Eleven-inch twin leading shoe (11in TLS) – front axle on 109in vehicles and 88in 1980 onwards. 6-cylinder and V8 models have wider brake shoes and drums, and a slightly different design of cylinder.

The 11in TLS front brake is often fitted as an upgrade to older 88in vehicles. The 11in SLS rear brake should not be fitted to the rear of 88in vehicles as it causes the back wheels to lock up under braking, but is sometimes found. It also occasionally turns up on the front axle of older 88in vehicles, providing a useful increase in braking performance over the 10in SLS brake.

Except for the 11in TLS brake, shoes are handed and should always be fitted correctly. On the 10in SLS brake there is a post on the leading shoe (towards the front of the vehicle) that engages with the adjuster. The shoes on the 11in SLS brake look identical, but the adjuster post on the leading shoe is positioned slightly lower down than on the trailing shoe. These brakes are very frequently fitted with the shoes the wrong way round, making them impossible

Brake cylinder, drum and shoes ready to fit.

10in SLS brake assembly with hub removed to show how the springs should be fitted.

LARGEST SPACING TOWARDS FRONT OF VEHICLE

11in SLS brake assembly, showing correct positioning of springs.

11in TLS front brake showing how the springs attach to the shoes.

Copper grease should be applied to moving points on brake shoes, even when refitting old ones.

to adjust properly. Note the distance between the adjuster post and the oval hole above it: shoes should be fitted so that those with the greatest distance between these two points are towards the front of the vehicle.

Before fitting new shoes, check that the adjusters are free to move and not excessively worn. The ends of the shoes, the edge of the adjuster and the contact point between shoes and backplate should be given a thin smear of copper grease. The locating slots for the ends of the shoes should be cleaned out so that the shoes do not stick. Return springs should be in good condition, not stretched or excessively rusted. It is vital that they are fitted correctly. The usual mistakes that people make are:

◆ Fitting the springs on the wrong side of the shoes. They should be fitted between the shoes and the backplate, so that they pull the shoes inwards against the backplate.
◆ Incorrect fitting of the upper spring on 10in SLS brakes. It should hook over the end of the adjuster post on the leading shoe, run underneath the adjuster (between the snail cam and the backplate) and then hook to the post on the backplate beneath the wheel cylinder. Mechanics accustomed to car-type brakes often attach this spring across the two shoes, not realizing that the trailing shoe

is supposed to be self-adjusting. They then wonder why the brake pedal goes almost to the floor.
◆ Fitting the springs to the wrong end of the shoes on 11in TLS brakes. They should attach to the end furthest from the piston, with the other end of each spring hooked around the post on the backplate.

This brake drum is badly scored and should be replaced.

Bleeding a new brake cylinder.

Good-quality brake shoes should be correctly profiled to fit new drums, but cheap shoes are often manufactured on the assumption that they will be fitted to badly worn drums, and if fitted in conjunction with new drums, they will lock up solid. This can be rectified by fitting the drum, turning the hub (using a lever, if necessary), removing the drum and sanding down the high spots where the drum has marked the shoe, then repeating the process until the drum clears the shoe. This can be a long, slow process.

REPLACING WHEEL CYLINDERS

The wheel cylinders on all of these vehicles are secured to the backplate with two 5/16in UNF nuts and spring washers, which should ideally be replaced with new ones. It is just about possible to replace the cylinders without removing the shoes on the SLS-type brakes but on the 11in TLS brake, the shoe trailing ends engage in slots in the cylinders, so the shoes must be removed to change the cylinders. The biggest obstacle tends to be the union securing the brake pipe to the cylinder. This either rounds off (using a flare nut spanner should prevent this) or is corroded to the brake pipe and twists it off when undone. You should be prepared to replace the brake pipe as well as the cylinder, and have new pipes to hand before starting the job. Note also that the original TRW/Girling cylinders have a conical centre to the inlet and require a double-flared pipe end, whereas most other makes of cylinder use single-flared pipes. Pipe unions on wheel cylinders are Imperial (3/8in × 24 TPI) in all cases.

There are two different types of SLS cylinder, which are of different diameters (1in/25.4mm and 1⅛in/30.7mm) but physically interchangeable. It is sadly very common for the wrong type to have been fitted. The cylinders are also handed left and right. The larger cylinders are fitted on the rear brakes of all vehicles with 11in TLS front brakes, and the front of 88in vehicles with 10in SLS front brakes. The smaller cylinders are for the rear of 88in vehicles with 10in SLS brakes all round. The cylinder diameter is normally cast into the body of the cylinder, or can be measured by peeling back the dust cover on one end. If doing this, ensure that the piston does not pop out of the cylinder, as there is a spring inside. 11in TLS cylinders are all the same diameter, but 6-cylinder and V8 models have a slightly different body and longer end to the piston and are not interchangeable with the 4-cylinder type.

REPLACING BRAKE PIPES AND HOSES

Brake fluid is taken from the master cylinder to the wheel cylinders by a mixture of rigid and flexible pipes. The rigid pipes were originally made of steel and corrode over time:

Bulge in this hose is caused by a failure of the inner layer. This is dangerous and should be replaced.

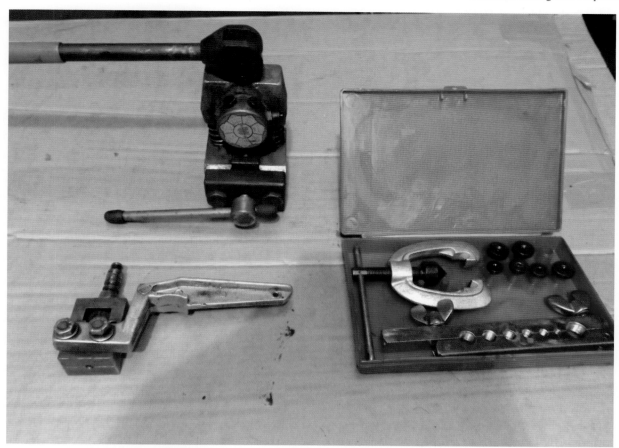

Brake pipe flaring tools, clockwise from top left: Wurth vice-mounted professional, cheap clamp-type, Moprod.

they are usually replaced with copper, which is much easier to shape. Brake pipes can be purchased ready-made, or made up using copper brake pipe, unions and a flaring tool. Professional-quality flaring tools are very expensive but cheap clamp-type tools seldom produce good, smooth flares. Probably the best flaring tool for the home-mechanic was the old Moprod design – these have been unavailable new for many years but it is worth trying to track one down if you plan to make your own pipes.

There are two kinds of pipe flare: single and double. The single flare has a rounded end and is designed to fit into a female conical seat in conjunction with a male pipe union. The double flare has the end splayed out like a trumpet to fit over a male conical seat. It is normally used in conjunction with a female pipe union to attach a rigid pipe to the end of a flexible hose but TRW/Girling wheel cylinders use a double flare with a male union, as do the three-way connectors at the front and back of pre-1980 Land Rovers. At some point during 1980, Land Rover changed from Imperial to metric unions for flexible brake pipes and three-way connectors, while still retaining Imperial unions for wheel cylinders. This can lead to a whole lot of fun when trying to work out which kind of hose and union to use. Imperial and metric unions are fairly close in dimensions, but not close enough to make a secure, safe connection.

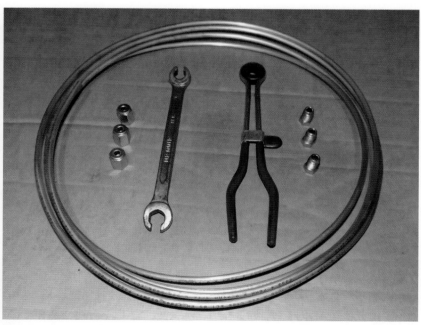

Flare spanner, hose clamp, copper pipe and unions.

Rigid brake lines should be routed to avoid contact with moving parts, and securely fixed using proper brake pipe clips (or cable ties for the pipes that run across the rear axle) at intervals of no more than 45cm (18in). Flexible hoses should be fitted with new nuts and star washers and not twisted along their length. When attaching a rigid pipe to a flexible hose, hold the end of the hose stationary with a spanner when tightening the union to avoid twisting the pipe. On older vehicles, the front hoses attach direct to the wheel cylinders with a copper sealing washer, which should always be replaced, ditto the rear hose where it screws into the three-way connector on pre-1980 vehicles.

REPLACING MASTER CYLINDERS

On vehicles fitted with a brake servo, this job could not be easier, as the two securing nuts are readily accessible. Being protected from road spray, the pipe unions usually come undone with no trouble. If making up new pipes on vehicles with dual-circuit brakes, note that the front chamber on the rear cylinder should connect to the rear-braking circuit and vice versa. The front and rear chambers have differently sized unions, so this will only be a problem if you have removed and thrown away the pipes before changing the master cylinder.

On non-servo vehicles, the master cylinder is bolted to the rear of the pedal box, and the lower securing nut and bolt are very hard to reach. You will find it much easier to remove the pedal box from the vehicle: it is retained with six bolts inside the footwell. The critical point is to ensure that the master cylinder pushrod is adjusted correctly, so that there is a small amount of free play at the end of the travel. On pre-1967 vehicles with a hydraulic brake light switch (mounted on a four-way connector on top of the chassis just forward of the bulkhead), the pushrod adjustment can be made with the pedal box off the vehicle. Later

vehicles use the brake light switch (mounted inside the footwell) as a pedal stop, and on these the pushrod length cannot be set until the pedal box and switch have been refitted. If there is no free play in the pushrod with the pedal at the top of its travel, the brakes will tend to 'pump up' and lock on with repeated use.

Non-servo vehicles have two different designs of master cylinder: the earlier CB-type, which has a cast-iron body with a large hexagon-headed plug at the end, and the later, simpler CV-type. Either type will fit the pedal box, but the inlet and outlet port positions are reversed. The outlet pipe (to the wheel cylinders) can normally be bent carefully to suit the new position, but the inlet pipe from the reservoir will need to be replaced. Good-quality CB master cylinders are now getting hard to obtain, but several specialists offer a reconditioning service, which involves relining the cylinder with a stainless-steel sleeve for long life.

STEERING – AN OVERVIEW

The steering system on all Series II, IIA and III vehicles is fundamentally the same, consisting of:

◆ a one-piece steering box and column assembly bolted to the bulkhead, transferring movement via a cast drop arm to
◆ a longitudinal steering tube with a ball-joint at each end, which connects to
◆ a steering relay, bolted through the front crossmember, transmitting steering movement through 90 degrees to
◆ a drag link, another straight tube with a ball-joint at each end, which connects to
◆ a steering swivel assembly at one end of the front axle, with
◆ a track rod, yet another straight tube with a ball-joint at each end, connecting the two swivel assemblies so that both front wheels turn together.

Steering rods – drag link and track rod.

Even when new, the steering was not especially precise, and once a little wear gets into each of the components, it can become very woolly indeed. Play can be detected by getting an assistant to turn the steering wheel back and forth through around 90 degrees while observing each component and joint in turn. The most common wear points are the six ball-joints, the steering relay and the steering swivel-pivots (covered in Chapter 10). Steering boxes are long-lasting and seldom cause problems if kept topped up with oil. However, as leaks from the output shaft seal are endemic to this design, boxes are quite often run dry, causing terminal wear to the internals.

BALL-JOINT REPLACEMENT

Each steering tube assembly consists of a hollow steel tube threaded at each end, two ball-joints with threaded ends and two clamps to prevent the threaded joints from turning in the tube. One end has a conventional right-handed thread, the other left-handed, so that the effective length of the assembly can be varied by loosening the clamps and turning the tube to enable adjustment. It follows that when replacing a ball-joint, the tube at the opposite end should be free to turn, allowing the steering to be adjusted once the assembly is refitted to the vehicle. This is where the trouble begins: the threaded ends of the joints are normally rusted solidly into the tube.

Faced with a vehicle where the ball-joints have not been disturbed for many years, the easiest solution is to buy a new tube, joints, clamps and bolts. Whether you do this or try to reclaim the old tube, the starting point is to remove the tube assembly. The joints are secured to the cast arms at either end via a tapered pin and either a castellated nut and split pin or a Nyloc nut. If you are planning to replace the joint, do not waste too much time trying to extract the split pin, as it will probably be rusted solid. Just snip the ends off, hammer a socket over the nut and give it a good heave with a breaker bar. The pin is not very strong. The taper joint then has to be broken, for which you will need a ball-joint separator, ideally of the 'scissor' type. Note that these joints are rather larger than those on most cars, so make sure that the separator you buy is large enough to cope. If you do not have a separator, the taper can usually be shocked free using the two hammers method: take a heavy club hammer in each hand and hit the steering arm simultaneously with both hammers on either side of the pin. This requires a certain amount of coordination but will usually free the joint after two or three sharp blows. Trying to free the joint by hitting the threaded end is usually a waste of time.

With the assembly on the bench, loosen the clamp bolts (they usually shear, so have replacements to hand), tap the clamps up towards the centre of the tube, then place the end of the tube on a flat, heavy steel surface and belt the outside of the tube with a hammer all the way around for a length of about 100mm (4in) from the end of the tube. Clamp the tube in a strong vice, slip a length of strong steel tube over the end of the taper pin and try to unscrew it. Of course you do not know at this point whether it has a left- or right-handed thread, so try both ways. With luck the

Scissor-type ball-joint separator.

joint will now unscrew from the tube. Clean up the two slots in the end of the tube, inspect the threads inside the tube to ensure they are not too badly corroded to be safe, give the threads of the new ball-joint a good coating of copper grease and wind it into the tube (ensuring, of course, that you have selected the joint with the correct handed thread for the tube). Then repeat for the other end and refit the assembly. Adjust to length and tighten the clamps.

Note that the design of ball-joint and tube end changed during the course of production, sometime in the early 1970s. Earlier ball-joints had a plain, unthreaded section at the inner end, with a corresponding plain section just inside the inner end of the tube. Later ball-joints and tubes were fully threaded. The later joint will fit the earlier tube and still clamp tight (provided the slots in the end of the tube are clear of rust and dirt) but the earlier joint will not fit the later tube.

STEERING RELAY

The steering relay has two functions: to transmit the steering action through 90 degrees, and to provide a degree of friction, preventing steering kickback and shimmy over rough surfaces. It consists of a substantial steel shaft, splined at each end, mounted in a heavy cast housing, with plain brass bearings top and bottom and two friction bushes bearing on tapered surfaces on the shaft inside the housing, with a very strong steel spring between them to force the bushes against the shaft. The housing is filled with oil: the bottom seal deteriorates over time, the oil leaks out and then either the shaft binds on the bearings (giving very heavy steering, which will not self-centre) or the bearings wear so that the shaft moves from side to side when the steering wheel is turned.

Steering-relay replacement is one of those jobs that even an experienced Land Rover mechanic dreads. The relay is a fairly close fit inside a steel tube that runs through the front crossmember, and the relay body rusts solidly to the tube. Although it is theoretically possible to rebuild a relay *in situ*, the strong internal spring makes dismantling and reassembly very hazardous indeed – even if you have the correct tools and know what you are doing. It is quite often necessary to cut large sections out of the crossmember to release the old relay, then weld everything back together before fitting the new one. However, relays can sometimes be salvaged without complete dismantling. Remove the bottom steering arm followed by the clamp ring and bottom bearing plate (four bolts each). Remove two of the top plate bolts (tricky to access) and then spray lots of WD40 into each of the bolt holes, and up into the relay internals from the bottom. Work the steering back and forth while repeatedly spraying in WD40. Then refit the bottom plate with a new bearing and seal (having cleaned up the surface of the shaft where the seal bears on it), refit the clamp ring and trickle EP90 gear oil through one of the top bolt holes until it emerges from the other. Refit the two top bolts and, with a new Nyloc nut, the bottom steering arm, and thoroughly tighten.

STEERING BOX

There are three different variants. Series II and IIA to the end of 1966 had a large sprung-spoke steering wheel secured to the column with a pinch bolt and nut. Later Series IIAs had a solid-spoke steering wheel attached to the column with a large central nut. The Series III used the same steering wheel, but with a different (spring-loaded) upper column bearing and a slot in the column tube for the steering lock mechanism. Play in the steering mechanism can be adjusted via a square-headed adjuster and large locknut on the outer face of the steering box, which is normally concealed by a box-shaped steel cover under the wing.

The seal on the output shaft is inadequate and often leaks. It can be replaced with the box *in situ*, after removing the cover plate and drop arm, and withdrawing the sector shaft. Anything more serious will normally require the box to be removed from the vehicle, which is a fairly involved operation. On the Series III, the ignition lock is clamped to the column with shear bolts, which will need to be drilled out, and removal of the drop arm from the sector shaft on all Series vehicles is almost impossible without the correct tool.

SUSPENSION

The suspension system on all these vehicles is delightfully simple. It consists of four multi-leaf 'cart' springs, each one bolted directly to the chassis at the front and via a swinging shackle at the back, clamped to the axles via heavy cast plates and 'U' bolts, with damping via telescopic oil-filled shock absorbers mounted between chassis and axles. Many of these vehicles ride very badly indeed, but this will usually be caused by springs that are either rusted solid or of the wrong specification for the vehicle. Springs will require replacement if the vehicle leans or sags badly, if the rust between the spring leaves is forcing them apart and bending the spring clamps, or if one or more leaves has broken.

Spring replacement is an arduous job due to the weight of the components. It is best to replace one spring at a time, loosening the 'U' bolts on the opposite side slightly so that the axle can be moved to locate the pin in the centre of the

Standard leaf spring in good condition with no signs of rust spreading the leaves apart.

Front spring shackles fitted correctly with the bosses at the bottom.

spring into the hole on the underside of the axle. The long bolts that secure the springs to the chassis pass through rubber bushes with steel centres, into which the bolts often rust solid. You may find it is necessary to cut through the bolts with a thin cutting disc in an angle grinder, then remove the chassis bushes (a horrible job, especially with the remains of a bolt stuck in them) and fit new ones. Some helpful tips:

◆ Support the vehicle on long axle stands placed underneath the chassis. Allow the axle to drop to full extension (with the shock absorbers removed), then jack it up about an inch and support it with shorter axle stands.

◆ Before undoing spring and 'U' bolt nuts, use an angle grinder to cut the ends off flush with the nut. This will save you a lot of effort trying to force nuts over rusty threads.

◆ When replacing front springs, disconnect the front propshaft at one end before starting the job. The sliding splines on the propshaft do not always have enough travel to allow the axle to move forwards far enough with the springs at full extension.

◆ Always fit new 'U' bolts, spring bolts and shackles, and use plenty of copper grease on the bolts.

◆ On the rear axle all four 'U' bolts are the same. On the front, the offside inner 'U' bolt is longer than the others and should have a square profile to match that of the axle casing.

◆ Before fitting each new spring, ensure that the locating hole on the underside of the axle is clear of rust so that the pin in the spring will locate properly in it.

◆ Make sure the front shackles are fitted the right way up: they have bosses on the inner face which should be at the bottom, with the plain ends at the top.

◆ Do not fully tighten the spring bolts and nuts until the vehicle is back on its wheels and sitting level.

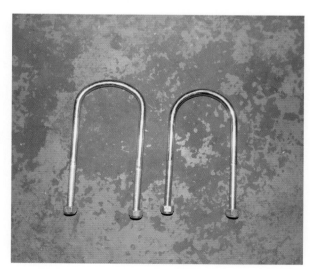

Front axle 'U' bolts: the longer, squarer one should be on the offside nearest the centre of the vehicle.

This rusted shock absorber retaining pin will need to be cut off and drilled out.

New split pin with copper grease.

Shock absorbers should be replaced if the outside of the casing is damp with fluid. Due to the stiffness of the suspension it is not possible to test them for correct operation by 'bouncing' the vehicle at each corner, but internal failures are rare and they will normally perform just fine until the fluid leaks out. They are attached using a long bolt and nut at the top, and either a washer and split pin or (on 109in vehicles) a nut and threaded stud through the axle casing at the bottom. The bottom mounts on vehicles with the washer/split pin system are often badly worn, so that the bushes do not compress enough to stop the shock absorber from flapping around. These can sometimes be salvaged by putting a second large washer over the first. On 109in vehicles it is essential that the washers and rubber bushes are correctly fitted: the two washers either side of the axle mount have a steel ring on them that locates in the hole in the bracket, preventing the threaded stud from rubbing against the hole and wearing it away. Before fitting, shock absorbers should be held vertically and worked up and down four or five times to expel any air.

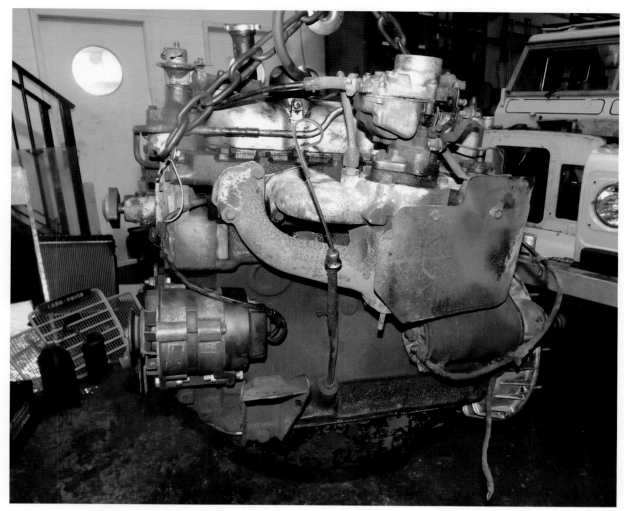

2.25 petrol engine on the crane.

engine and related systems

Engine repairs can be broadly divided into two types: those that can be accomplished with the engine in the vehicle and those for which the engine will need to be removed. Engine removal might seem a daunting prospect, but thanks to the

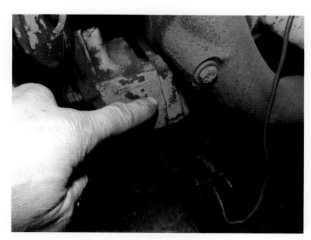

Usual engine number location on 2286cc engines.

simplicity of old Land Rover engines and the large amount of space within the engine bay, it is well within the capabilities of any moderately competent home-mechanic. Major tasks that can be accomplished with the engine in the vehicle include the removal of the cylinder head, front timing cover (for access to the timing chain and camshaft) and sump (allowing removal of the oil pump). The engine will need to be removed to replace the crankshaft rear oil seal.

CYLINDER COMPRESSION TESTING

The most common reasons for wishing to remove the cylinder head (or heads on a V8, which has two) are either head-gasket failure or burned exhaust valves. Symptoms of head-gasket failure can take several forms. On Land Rover engines, what is usually thought of as a 'classic' failure (across one of the waterways, resulting in coolant loss and overheating) is relatively uncommon, as there is a lot of metal around the water passages between block and head. More likely is that the gasket will fail between two

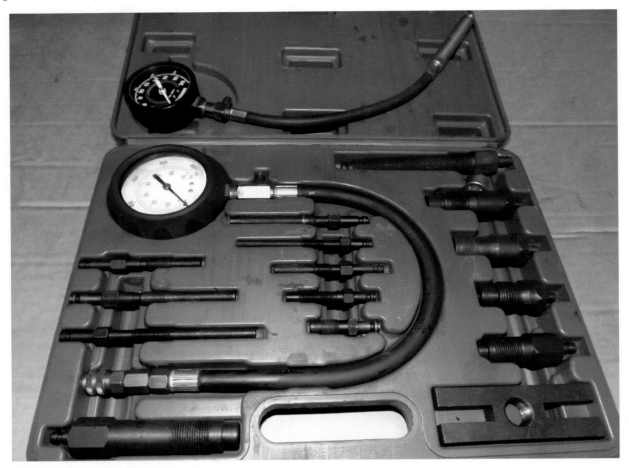

Compression testers for petrol and diesel engines.

adjacent cylinders (leading to very rough running and loss of power) or, on 4-cylinder engines (and especially diesels), between one of the cylinders and a pushrod tube, which pressurizes the crankcase and blows oil everywhere. V8 engines have no waterways between the front and rear of the head, and the gaskets tend to weaken along the inner edge of the head, leading to a slight loss of compression and filling the engine with soot. Loss of compression can also be due to burnt valves (usually caused by running on unleaded fuel without a lead substitute additive) or, more rarely, a cracked cylinder head, or a cracked or holed piston.

If a failed head-gasket is suspected, the first task is to carry out a compression test. Compression testers for petrol engines are fairly cheap and consist of a gauge mounted to a flexible hose with a threaded fitting on the end. The spark plugs are removed and the gauge screwed into each plug hole in turn. With the ignition system disconnected by pulling the high-tension lead off the coil, crank the engine over on the starter with the throttle pedal fully depressed for five or six revolutions, then check the gauge reading. All cylinders should give a compression figure within 10 per cent of each other. The actual figure is less important, but on a healthy engine you should see around 140–160psi depending on the compression ratio. A reading much below 130psi would suggest that the cylinder bores and pistons are fairly worn – the engine will be down on power and burning some oil.

Compression testers for diesel engines are more expensive as they have to cope with far higher pressures. They come with a selection of adapters for different engines. The glow plugs should be removed and the tester connected to each cylinder in turn, using the appropriate adapter. The compression test must be carried out with the engine shut-off in the 'stop' position. Note that on the Series III, if the engine stop knob is pulled out, it will automatically spring back in when the key is turned to the start position, so the stop cable will need to be disconnected at the pump end and the lever physically secured in the 'off' position using a spring or cable tie. On earlier vehicles, it is sufficient to ensure that the stop knob is pulled fully out when operating the starter. Again, all compressions should be within 10 per cent of each other. Actual figures vary depending on the design of the tester but a 'typical' figure (measured at the glow plug aperture) would be around 430–460psi.

CYLINDER-HEAD REMOVAL AND REPLACEMENT

If the compression test reveals a significant variation between cylinders, it will be necessary to remove the cylinder head to establish the reason. This is not an especially difficult task: the main problems are that the head bolts are done up very tight, and the head itself (on 4- and 6-cylinder engines) is made of cast iron and very heavy indeed. V8 engines have aluminium heads, which can easily be lifted. You may also run into problems detaching the exhaust downpipe from the manifold. Land Rover originally specified deep brass securing nuts, but these are often replaced with steel. The studs themselves corrode and weaken, and it is highly likely that in attempting to remove the nuts, at least one of the studs will shear off. Broken studs can usually be repaired by drilling them out and fitting Helicoil inserts.

Cylinder head bolts should be loosened (and tightened again) in a very specific sequence, which is given in the workshop manual. They are loosened progressively from the outer ends of the engine towards the middle, and tightened from the middle outwards. Failure to observe this procedure may result in a cracked cylinder head. Make sure that you have detached the oil feed pipe at the back of the cylinder head (not present on V8 engines) before attempting to remove the head: this is often overlooked. With all the securing bolts removed, you will probably find that the head is still firmly stuck to the block. The seal can be broken by levering carefully between one of the parts of the head casting that protrude from the head and an adjacent part of the block. Do not under any circumstances attempt to insert a thin chisel or screwdriver directly between the mating faces of the head and block: you will damage both and possibly render your engine scrap. Make sure you have somewhere to rest the head (such as a thick sheet of corrugated card) before lifting it off the engine. It will still contain a significant amount of old oil, and must not be placed directly onto a concrete floor to avoid damage. Cast-iron heads will normally require two people to remove them safely.

With the head removed, the old head-gasket can be recovered and inspected for signs of damage. A major failure should be obvious. Most of these engines have metal-faced gaskets, which come off in one piece, but sometimes you will find these have been replaced with the later self-sealing composite gaskets, which break up on removal and have to be scraped off the block and head in bits. When doing this it is important to ensure that you do not gouge the mating faces of head and block, or drop little bits of gasket down the pushrod holes or waterways in the block. These should be temporarily plugged with pieces of paper towel before starting to clean up the block face.

The cylinder head should be cleaned up and carefully inspected for signs of cracking. Petrol engines sometimes crack on the edges of the combustion chambers, and if the crack spreads underneath the sealing ring on the head-gasket, the new gasket will probably fail within a short time. Diesels most commonly crack across the replaceable 'hot spots' (circular inserts that overlap the edge of the cylinder bores) and, more occasionally, across the face of the head between the valves and hot spots. Replacement of hot spots is best left to a machine shop as they need to be fitted within fairly precise tolerances. Ill-fitted hot spots can break up and drop into the cylinder with terminal consequences. V8s do not seem especially prone to cracking, being made of softer aluminium, but can corrode badly around the waterways between the head and block. If this corrosion extends underneath the head-gasket, the head is probably scrap, although light corrosion can sometimes be dealt with by having the head skimmed.

The cast-iron heads do not normally need to be skimmed (a machine-shop procedure that involves grinding the face of the head with a special machine so that it is perfectly flat and smooth) and can usually be cleaned up ready for refitting by scraping off gasket deposits and accumulated corrosion, then finishing off with 400 grade wet and dry paper. Aluminium heads tend to warp in service and it is always advisable to have them lightly skimmed, even if they appear to be perfectly flat. As well as external

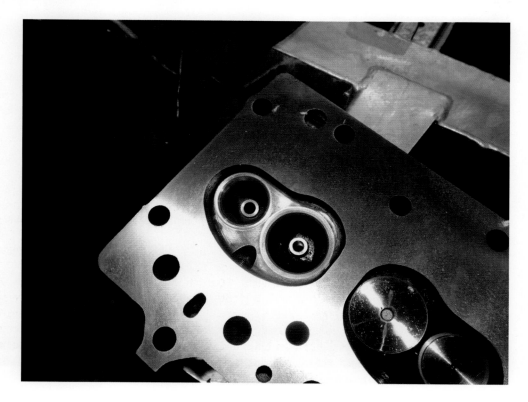

Cylinder head fresh from the machine shop, with hardened exhaust valve seats for unleaded fuel.

cracking, cylinder heads can suffer from internal cracks, which can only be detected by pressure-testing. If there is any suspicion that the head might be cracked internally (for example, unexplained coolant loss or a tendency to build up pressure in the cooling system), the head should be pressure-tested. Any machine shop that specializes in engine work should be able to do this at reasonable cost.

Whether you choose to remove the valves for inspection will to some extent depend on the nature of the problem you are trying to rectify. If it is a straightforward head-gasket failure and the engine was previously running just fine, you might think it is not worth the trouble of removing the valves, for which a valve spring compressor is required. However, the valve stem oil seals (which prevent oil from running down the valves and into the cylinders) tend to harden with age and become ineffective, and cannot easily be replaced without removing the head. Removal of the valves will also give you the opportunity to check the condition of the valves, seats and guides: valves and seats on petrol engines can become badly pitted, and guides can also wear badly.

Valve-seat pitting is invariably caused by running an unmodified engine on unleaded fuel without a suitable additive. On the 4-cylinder petrol engines, the valve seats are machined directly into the relatively soft cast-iron cylinder head. In the old days, petrol contained tetra-ethyl lead, which acted as a lubricant, protecting the exhaust valve seats and preventing the valves from sticking to them. Lead as a fuel additive was banned many years ago, and engines made since that time have hardened inserts in the valve seats to protect them. Without these inserts, every time an exhaust valve closes and then opens, a microscopic fragment of metal is torn away from the seat. Over time the seat becomes rough and pitted, so that the valve no longer seals properly. Eventually, the passage of hot gases past the ill-sealing valve starts to eat away at the valve head itself, leading fairly quickly to total loss of compression.

For this reason, it is not recommended to run an unmodified 4-cylinder petrol engine in a Land Rover Series II, IIA or III on unleaded fuel unless a lead-replacement additive is mixed with the fuel. 6-cylinder and V8 engines are already fitted with hardened valve seats and can tolerate unleaded fuel without problems. Modifying a 4-cylinder head to cope with unleaded is a fairly straightforward job for a machine shop: the old valve seats are machined out and new hardened seats pressed in, along with new valves and guides. A fair number of older Land Rovers have already been modified, but the only way to tell whether this has been done is to remove an exhaust valve and inspect the seat carefully. If the original seat has been machined out and an insert pressed in, there will be an obvious ring round the seat and a change in the graining of the metal. If you find that your head does not have hardened inserts, it makes sense either to have them fitted or to buy a reconditioned cylinder head that has already been modified to suit unleaded fuel.

Refitting a cylinder head is fairly straightforward. Follow the procedures in the workshop manual – especially the sequence for tightening the head bolts. You will need a good-quality ½in drive torque wrench. Although the work-

These heat-sensitive tabs indicate a head that has been rebuilt and is probably unleaded-compatible.

Composite (top) and copper head-gaskets for a 2.25 engine.

shop manual for most variants of these engines gives only a single torque figure, it is best to tighten them sequentially in two stages: initially to half the specified torque setting, and then fully tight, following the recommended tightening sequence at each stage. The head-gaskets originally specified were made of copper on 4- and 6-cylinder engines, and pressed steel on V8s. Modern alternatives use a self-sealing composite material: these usually last far longer and are better at sealing any minor imperfections in the mating surfaces.

Head-gaskets should always be fitted 'dry', i.e. without any kind of sealing compound, and the faces of head and block must be perfectly clean and dry. Cylinder head bolts on 4- and 6-cylinder engines can be reused unless rusty or damaged. Those on V8s are much weaker and quite often snap if reused, so should be replaced with new ones. Composite gaskets on V8s sometimes lack the necessary bolt holes for the short bolts on the outer edges of the head: these bolts can safely be left out as they tend to pull the inner edge of the head away from the block. If using the older type of gasket, these outer bolts should only be tightened to 20lb ft (2.8kg m), regardless of what your workshop manual may tell you.

Before refitting the head, check that the threaded head bolt holes in the block are clean and empty of fluid and debris. If one of them contains oil or water, attempting to tighten the head bolt against the fluid creates a very

effective home-made hydraulic ram, which can crack the cylinder block. Ensure that the head-gasket is fitted the right way up: some are marked 'TOP' on the upper face, but by no means all are. If in doubt, look at the holes on the gasket for the water passages – those towards the front of the engine will be smaller than those at the back – to ensure that the rear of the engine (furthest away from the water pump) receives the same amount of coolant flow as the front.

On petrol engines there is no provision to locate the gasket accurately on the block before lowering the head onto it. The solution is to take two spare cylinder head bolts, cut the heads off them and then cut a slot into them to take a screwdriver. These then act as temporary locating dowels. Screw them into two appropriate holes in the block, drop the head-gasket over them, lower the head into place and fit all the other head bolts, screwing them in hand-tight. Finally, remove the two temporary dowels and replace them with head bolts.

TIMING COVER AND SUMP

The main reasons why you might want to remove these are: to replace a sump damaged by over-enthusiastic off-roading, to replace the front crankshaft oil seal, or to attend to the timing chain and tensioner. The front end of the sump overlaps the timing cover, and removal of the timing

COMPRESSION RATIOS: WHICH DO YOU HAVE?

Both 4- and 6-cylinder engines were available in two compression ratios, with the lower being intended for use with poor-quality fuels. On the 6-cylinder engine, this was achieved through the use of different pistons and the specification can only be determined with reference to the engine number. On 4-cylinder engines, the 7:1 and 8:1 versions used different cylinder heads, and as Land Rover specified different spark plugs for the two variants, many new owners will wish to establish whether their engine is 7:1 or 8:1.

To identify the type, look at the area around the centre head bolt on the manifold side. If it has a flat, square area adjacent to it, the head might be of either type: carefully clean up the area and look for a number stamped faintly on it. An '8' indicates an 8:1 head; a '7' or no stamp will be 7:1. If there is no flat area at all, the head is 7:1. On later metric heads (identified by the casting number HRC1303), there may be a part number stamped on the flat instead. If it is ERC5900, it is a 7:1 head; anything else is 8:1 and ETC5412 is an 8:1 head from a 2.5 engine with hardened valve seats for unleaded fuel.

No raised square boss – 7:1 head.

Raised square boss – inspect stamped marks to determine head type.

cover inevitably damages the sump gasket, so if the timing cover is to be removed, the sump also has to come off. This is not a difficult job but the sump is attached with a large number of bolts. With these removed, a thin chisel is carefully inserted between sump and block to break the seal between the two. The sump can then be carefully lowered, manoeuvring it around the pickup strainer on the oil pump. It can then be cleaned out and all traces of gasket carefully removed from both sump and block. Thick, grey sludge in the bottom of the sump is a bad sign, as it will have come from the crankshaft bearings and indicates that a complete engine overhaul is imminent. Broken metal fragments in the sump are also not good, and it can be very hard to identify what they are and where they have come from.

The timing cover is again secured by a ring of bolts, some of which also pass through the water pump. These can be badly corroded and hard to remove (dealing with sheared-off bolts is a subject covered in Chapter 5). It is much easier to remove the radiator first, not least because it removes the risk of accidentally damaging it while working on the engine. The crankshaft pulley must be removed: the securing bolt is done up very tight and secured either with a locking tab or (on some later engines) Loctite on the thread. With the sump removed, a suitable hardwood block can be wedged between the crankshaft and the side of the block to lock the crank so that the bolt can be undone: the pulley can then usually be carefully levered off the end of the crankshaft. Inspect the area of the pulley shaft where the seal bears on it: if it is badly grooved, the pulley should be replaced.

On 4- and 6-cylinder engines, the crankshaft front oil seal sits behind a metal plate that is riveted to the timing case. If the plate and rivets are intact, the old seal can be removed (using a hook-type seal puller) from inside the case and a new seal pressed in. It helps to bevel the edge of the seal aperture using a grinding wheel in a mini-drill before fitting the new seal, so that the outer edge of the seal slips smoothly into the aperture and is not torn on the sharp edge. You will often find that someone has tried to replace the seal without removing the timing case by drilling out the rivets and then re-securing the plate with self-tapping screws. This usually ends up with one or more screws snapped off in the timing case, and extracting the remains of hardened self-tappers is no fun. You may end up having to drift them out with a parallel punch and hammer. If you wish to be able to replace the seal in future without having to remove the timing cover, the best approach is to drill and tap the holes to take M4 Allen screws.

The timing chain and tensioner on 4- and 6-cylinder petrol engines are under-stressed and long-lasting, and by the time they need attention, the rest of the engine will also be badly worn. V8 engines do not have a tensioner and the chain can become very stretched and baggy, although by this time the camshaft and followers will also be past their best. The whole lot can be replaced with the engine still in the vehicle, although this kind of major engine surgery is outside the scope of this book. Diesels have the same design of chain and tensioner as 4-cylinder petrol engines, but the chain also has to drive the injection pump (via a gear off the camshaft) and the extra load causes it

Timing marks on a 2.25 diesel injection pump.

to stretch, which affects the pump timing. For this reason the timing chain on a 2.25 diesel seldom lasts the life of the engine.

Replacing the timing chain on one of these engines is not technically difficult but can be time-consuming. The teeth on the chainwheels (camshaft, crankshaft and tensioner) tend to wear with the chain and should always be replaced at the same time, and this is where the trouble starts. The camshaft chainwheel has six possible positions on the camshaft, and must be fitted so that number one exhaust valve is fully open when the 'EP' mark on the flywheel is aligned with the pointer (visible through the timing window on the top of the flywheel housing). To achieve this you will need a dial test gauge bearing on the valve rocker for number one exhaust valve. The only way to achieve the correct setting is to fit the chainwheel, tensioner and chain, check the marks and if the timing is not spot-on, remove the chainwheel from the camshaft and try another position. Half a tooth out is not good enough. And once you have the camshaft timing exactly right, the injection pump timing will need to be reset. Depending on the age of your injection pump, you may need a special Land Rover tool to do this, although on most pumps the timing can be set accurately by removing the inspection window on the side of the pump and aligning the marks as per the workshop manual.

When refitting the timing cover and sump, it goes without saying that new gaskets should be used. The timing cover on 4-cylinder engines has two: a large one around the main cover and a smaller one around the water passage on the right-hand side of the block. A smear of Blue Hylomar on both mating faces will help to ensure a good seal, as well as keeping the gaskets in place while you manoeuvre the cover into place. The bolts should be given a coating of copper grease, and any corroded bolts should be replaced with new ones. Spring washers should always be renewed.

One useful tip is to make sure that the woodruff key on the end of the crankshaft is in the 12 o'clock position before you fit the cover: it can sometimes drop out when attempting to slide the pulley over it. The pulley should be refitted and the bolt tightened (again using a block of hardwood to lock the engine) before refitting the sump. Either use a new locking tab or Loctite to stop the securing bolt from coming undone, and make sure it is done up nice and tight.

ENGINE REMOVAL AND CRANKSHAFT REAR OIL SEAL REPLACEMENT

There are normally two reasons why you might want to remove the engine: either to replace it with another one (or completely rebuild it) or to replace a leaking rear crankshaft oil seal. It is not uncommon on old Land Rovers to find engine oil dripping out of the drain hole on the bottom of the flywheel housing: this makes a nasty mess on the driveway, is bad for the environment and, if left for long enough, will contaminate the clutch with oil. To access the oil seal, the engine and gearbox must be separated. Although it is technically possible to do this job by removing the gearbox and leaving the engine in the vehicle, you will find it much easier to accomplish if the engine is removed instead, especially on 6-cylinder engines and pre-1980 'fours' with the three-bearing crankshaft, where the sump and rear main bearing cap have to come off to change the seal.

To remove the engine you will need a suitable engine crane and lifting chain. The 4- and 6-cylinder engines sit a long way back in the engine bay and you will need a long-reach crane, unless you fancy removing the front bumper. A further advantage of a long-reach crane is that it will lift the engine high enough to clear the radiator panel, avoiding the need to disturb the bird's nest of fragile wiring that runs across it. The radiator will still have to come out. On

Using a long-reach crane the engine can normally be removed without disturbing the front panel.

4- and 6-cylinder vehicles, you will need to remove the floor panels and both parts of the transmission tunnel: these are held on with a large number of rusty screws and bolts, and you may have to resort to the use of an angle grinder. The engine on a 109 V8 can be removed without having to take the floors or transmission tunnel out. Then it is simply a question of disconnecting everything that attaches the engine to the vehicle, not forgetting the choke cable (petrol engines) or engine stop cable (diesels) and the earth strap that runs between the engine and chassis, usually attached at one end to the starter motor.

Damaged piston on a 2.25 diesel: the top ring shattered and fragments ended up embedded in the piston crown. It still ran, but not very well.

On most 4- and 6-cylinder engines, the lifting eyes are very small and will not take a 'D' shackle. These can be removed and either replaced with the larger lifting plates from a later engine or the ends of the chain bolted direct to the engine, using suitable bolts and large, thick washers. V8s have large lifting eyes front and back. Make sure you attach the crane to the lifting chain with a 'D' shackle passing through the chain at the mid-point, so that the engine lifts level and does not slip on the chain. Engine-mounting rubbers should be undone top and bottom. On 4- and 6-cylinder engines, the mount on one side is fitted to a wedge-shaped bracket that is bolted to the chassis: the bottom nut for the mounting rubber cannot be accessed, so the bracket should be unbolted from the chassis instead. Take the weight of the engine on the crane, carefully lift it until the brackets are clear of the rubbers, then carefully pull it forwards clear of the bellhousing studs and slowly lift it out, repeatedly checking that no part of the engine is catching on any pipes, cables or other items in the engine bay. It will be much safer and easier if you have an assistant to help you. Once the engine is clear of the engine bay, it can be gently lowered to the floor. You will need to place a large wooden block under the front to stop it from tipping forwards.

To replace the crankshaft oil seal, the clutch, flywheel, starter motor and flywheel housing (except on V8s) will have to be removed. On some engines the sump also has to come off. This can, in theory, be done with the engine dangling from a crane, but this is not even remotely safe,

Diagonal reinforcing webs indicate a five-bearing engine block.

and the engine should be mounted on a suitable purpose-made engine stand. If such a stand is not available, you may be able to get away with thoroughly draining all fluids, removing the manifolds, rolling the engine onto its side (for which you will definitely need an assistant) and supporting it with wooden blocks. This is not the recommended way of doing things but it is a lot safer than having the hydraulics on your engine crane fail while you are directly underneath the engine trying to remove the rear main bearing cap.

The exact method of replacing the seal will depend on the type of engine. The basic procedure is covered in the workshop manual, but the following points are worth highlighting.

Split Seals (4-Cylinder with Three-Bearing Crankshaft and 6-Cylinder Engines)

The seal has a split in the circumference so that it can be opened out to pass over the crankshaft journal. It is then held together with a hooked spring. The split in the seal must be positioned at the top of the engine, and great care taken to ensure that the spring is correctly located inside the recess in the seal. There are two crescent-shaped retainers that bolt to the back of the engine: these are rubber-coated, harden with age and should always be replaced. When refitting the rear main bearing cap, the cork 'T' seals must be renewed, otherwise they will leak oil, which will make the entire operation pointless. To do this you will need to either acquire or make up a pair of seal guides that bolt to the block and prevent the cork seals from being torn as the bearing cap is pushed home. Before tightening the bearing cap and seal retainer bolts, the seal should be carefully checked to ensure that it is sitting absolutely square and level in the retainers.

One-Piece Seals (4-Cylinder Engines with Five-Bearing Crankshaft)

With the flywheel housing removed, the seal can be knocked out from behind with a chisel, taking great care not to mark the housing. There are two types of seal: the older rubber-cased seal is now obsolete and should be replaced with the later metal-cased version (ERR2532). This comes with a plastic guide that slips over the end of the crankshaft to protect the lip of the seal. The seal housing must be completely clean and dry, and the new seal must be pressed in squarely using a ring of the correct size, not bashed in with a hammer and drift. These seals are very fragile and will fail if the outer casing is distorted. There is a large 'O' ring on the back face of the flywheel housing, which must always be renewed before fitting the housing to the block. When refitting the flywheel housing, it should be carefully offered up so that the plastic guide fits over the end of the crankshaft and the two locating dowels in the block engage with the holes in the housing. Push the housing squarely onto the dowels until the securing bolts engage with the threads in the block, then tighten the bolts slowly and progressively to draw the housing squarely onto the block. Once the seal has passed over the end of the crankshaft, the plastic guide will pop out and can be discarded. When refitting the flywheel, the bolts should be treated with thread locking/sealing fluid, otherwise oil will migrate along the threads and contaminate the clutch.

V8 Engines

These use a one-piece rubber seal that is pressed into a recess in the back of the engine block. To remove the old seal, drill two small holes in it at 180-degree spacing to take self-tapping screws: grasp these with self-grip pliers and pull the seal out. The new seal should be carefully tapped in using a metal ring of the correct size, taking great care not to damage the lip of the seal when sliding it over the end of the crankshaft.

Engine Refitting

It is important to ensure that the clutch plate is centralized on the flywheel (this procedure is covered in Chapter 9). On Series III vehicles, the clutch release bearing should be replaced as a matter of course, and the pivot points for the clutch fork and pushrod greased. The end of the gearbox

input shaft, including the splines, should also be given a light smear of grease. The engine must be supported by a crane so that it is level in both planes. If the back of the engine does not meet the bellhousing squarely, the gearbox input shaft will not engage with the clutch plate. If the engine does not slide easily onto the gearbox, try engaging a gear and then turning the crankshaft using a spanner or socket on the retaining bolt, until the splines on the input shaft engage with those in the clutch. If the gearbox mounting rubbers are badly perished or broken, attempting to slide the engine onto the gearbox will simply result in the gearbox being pushed backwards in the chassis.

Home-made seal guides to aid refitting the rear main bearing cap.

Series III transmission: remarkably compact by modern standards.

9

clutch and transmission

Apart from the 109 V8, all of these vehicles share a broadly similar transmission setup, with a hydraulically operated clutch driving a four-speed manual gearbox, which in turn feeds power to a two-speed transfer box, which splits the drive between front and rear wheels. In normal road use, only the rear wheels are driven: selecting four-wheel drive locks the front and rear propshafts together, and selecting low ratio automatically engages four-wheel drive. The 109 V8 has a far more substantial gearbox (designated LT95 and based on the early Range Rover unit) in which four-wheel drive is permanently engaged, with the drive to the front axle feeding through a lockable differential unit built into the transfer box.

The gearboxes are all simple, old-fashioned units that can be rebuilt without the need for specialist tools; parts are readily and cheaply available. The V8 transmission has the main gearbox and transfer box built into a single casing. On the 4- and 6-cylinder vehicles, the gearbox and transfer box can be split and worked on separately. Clutches are simple and robust.

FAULT DIAGNOSIS

The standard four-speed gearbox actually started life in a Rover saloon car in 1937 and was arguably never quite strong enough for off-road use, despite many modifications during its long life. These gearboxes tend to be a little noisy, even when in good condition, and minor oil leaks are endemic. A slightly tired gearbox may continue to give good service for many years, if treated with some sympathy. The LT95 gearbox and the transfer boxes on both types of transmission are near enough unbreakable. The main problems that you are likely to find on the 4- and 6-cylinder gearboxes are:

◆ **Oil leaks:** endemic to these transmissions. Starting from the top, oil seeps from the seals on the selector shafts and detent springs, and runs down the sides of the casing. This is normal. The gasket between the bellhousing and main gearbox casing can fail with age, as can the one at the join between the gearbox and transfer box. The bottom cover plate on the transfer box is weak and tends to distort when the nuts are tightened, so leaks here are common. A cast aluminium replacement plate is available from Rocky Mountain. Transfer boxes usually weep some oil from the join between the casing and the rear output housing, as there is no gasket, just a stack of steel shims. Finally, the seals on the front and rear output flanges harden with age. Failure of the rear seal will contaminate the transmission brake with oil.

Four-wheel drive selector shafts are behind this pressed steel cover.

◆ **Reverse gear selection:** the reverse gear detent consists of a hinged flap and two springs attached to the reverse selector fork. When a spring breaks, the flap sticks up, allowing reverse to be engaged as easily as first. The springs can be replaced without too much trouble, but the floors and transmission tunnel have to come out.

◆ **Sticking transfer lever:** on vehicles where four-wheel drive and low ratio are infrequently used, the shafts inside the transfer box can stick. The usual symptom is that it becomes impossible to engage high ratio without also pushing down the yellow knob for four-wheel drive. The front ends of the shafts are concealed under a pressed steel cover on the front extension housing: if this is removed, lubricating the shafts and giving them a tap with a hammer, then working them back and forth, will usually restore normal operation.

◆ **Jammed gear lever:** the ball at the bottom end has a groove in it for an 'O' ring to stop it rattling. Sometimes a combination of missing 'O' ring, worn ball and worn forks allows the ball to slip between two of the forks, jamming the mechanism entirely. The floors and transmission tunnel will need to come out so the gear lever can be removed for attention. Gear levers can also break off at the bottom due to metal fatigue: it is not uncommon to find they have been welded back on.

◆ **'Crunching' between gears:** Series II and IIA gearboxes have no synchromesh on first or second gear, so you will need to master the double-declutching technique for crunch-free changes. Crunching on third and fourth gear is usually caused by failure of the flat metal springs in the third/fourth gear synchromesh hub: these are almost impossible to replace without stripping the gearbox, but

ABOVE: First/second synchromesh hub on the Series III gearbox often breaks here.

LEFT: Third/fourth synchromesh hub and one of the flat centralizing springs. These springs break quite often and end up in the bottom of the gearbox.

it will happily plod on like this for quite a while, provided you double-declutch and change gear slowly. First/second gear synchromesh hubs on Series III gearboxes have a weak spot where the synchromesh rings locate: the corners of the hub break off, eventually leading to a very notchy and obstructive selection of first and/or second gear. The synchromesh rings also wear with age and can be 'beaten' if changing gear too quickly.

Reverse idler gear and shaft showing fairly typical damage.

- ◆ **Reverse gear idler:** reverse is a straight-cut gear with no synchromesh. Repeated abuse (slamming the gear lever into reverse while still rolling forwards) will eventually break the teeth on the reverse idler. Gearboxes up to Series III Suffix A have a plain bushed idler, which gets very noisy with age. Suffix B and later have a roller-bearing idler, which should in theory be quieter. Many aftermarket roller-bearing idlers are incorrectly machined and will cause the gearbox to jump out of reverse; a modified idler is available from R. Whitehouse and Sons.

- ◆ **Layshaft failures:** Series II and IIA layshafts are attached to the front bearing with a nut and split pin, with the gears splined onto the shaft and sandwiched by a steel tube. This is a known weak point and, despite several redesigns during its life, the layshaft can break without warning, resulting in total gearbox failure. On the Series III, the layshaft is machined in one piece and seldom fails, but is retained in place with a Loctited bolt, which has a habit of coming loose, allowing the layshaft to move backwards and to destroy the

Layshafts compared: Series III above, Series II below.

rear bearing and gearbox case. If the engine and gearbox are split for any reason, it is worth removing the gearbox front cover (three bolts, four nuts) to check the layshaft bolt. If a gearbox is noisy in every gear except fourth, that points to a layshaft bearing problem.

Series III front cover is held on with four nuts and three bolts. The layshaft bolt, which often comes loose, is behind it.

On the Series II/IIA gearbox, the clutch release mechanism is built into the front cover.

◆ **Jumping out of forward gears:** quite common on old, worn gearboxes. If you are very lucky, a new set of detent springs in the top cover might cure the problem, but more usually it is down to wear on the dog teeth between the mainshaft gears and synchromesh hubs – caused by 'crunching' into gear on gearboxes with synchromesh problems. The teeth should be sharply pointed but on many older gearboxes they are worn down to round blobs. A full rebuild is the only way to rectify this fault. A badly worn spigot bush in the back of the flywheel can also cause gearboxes to jump out of fourth gear.

◆ **Gearbox noise:** most Series gearboxes, even freshly rebuilt ones, whine to some extent. It is a seventy-eight-year-old design after all. Excessive noise in every gear except top will be layshaft-related. On the 109 V8 gearbox, the layshaft runs on taper roller bearings, which are hard to set up accurately and tend to wear, so almost all of these gearboxes make a loud whirring noise in the lower gears. Noise in all gears is more likely to be mainshaft bearings. A regular rattle or clicking noise may be due to a broken gear tooth: the gears are strong but not indestructible. Noisy reverse gear is normally caused by wear in the idler bush/bearing and shaft: some replacement layshafts on later Series III gearboxes have the wrong tooth pitch on the reverse cog, and these will whine in reverse even when all components are brand new.

CLUTCHES

These usually have a very long life, being rather more substantial than those on most contemporary cars of similar size and weight. Eventually the friction lining on the clutch plate will wear down to the rivets and the clutch will slip under load, initially when accelerating in fourth gear. However, clutch slip can also result from incorrect adjustment of the clutch master cylinder pushrod, slave cylinder pushrod (on Series II and IIA transmissions) or internal collapse of the flexible hose between master and slave cylinder. Clutch judder may be due to the clutch being contaminated with oil, but is more often the result of the engine and gearbox mounting rubbers having failed. Clutch drag (failure to disengage fully) is usually caused by air in the hydraulic system or worn components in the clutch release mechanism on Series II and IIA vehicles. When diagnosing clutch problems, it makes sense to eliminate all other possible causes before condemning the clutch itself, as most clutch-related faults can be repaired without having to separate the engine and gearbox.

Clutch covers, clockwise from top left: Series II/IIA standard, Series IIA heavy-duty/diesel, Series III.

CLUTCH REPLACEMENT

The clutch itself consists of three components: the clutch plate (which is faced with friction material and transmits the drive from engine to gearbox), clutch cover (which presses the clutch plate against the flywheel) and release bearing (which pushes against the centre of the clutch cover to release the pressure on the clutch plate and disengage drive). When the clutch plate is badly worn, it and the cover should be replaced together. It is a false economy to replace the plate alone. On the Series III, the release bearing is a self-contained unit and should be replaced with the rest of the clutch. Series II and IIA have the release bearing built into the gearbox, and this should not need replacing unless it squeals when the clutch pedal is depressed, which is unusual.

4-cylinder petrol Series II and IIA vehicles and Series II diesels left the factory with a 9in diameter coil-spring clutch. Series IIA 6-cylinder and diesel models had a 9½in diaphragm spring clutch, which is not only stronger but lighter in operation. This was available as a factory option on the 4-cylinder petrol vehicles. The Series III standardized on the 9½in diaphragm clutch, and the 109 V8 had a 10½in diaphragm clutch throughout production. The 9in and 9½in clutches are more or less interchangeable, the main difference being that the larger clutch has three locating dowels on the flywheel 120 degrees apart, whereas the smaller one has two, 180 degrees apart. Most flywheels have holes drilled for both alternatives, so a 9½in clutch can be fitted in place of a 9in one by tapping new dowels into the appropriate holes and carefully drilling out the one redundant dowel. The flywheel bolt pattern for both clutches is identical. It is, however, important to ensure that the correct clutch cover is fitted for the type of clutch release mechanism. The Series IIA diesel clutch has a large triangular boss in the cover, which bears against the 'top hat' clutch release sleeve in the gearbox. The Series III clutch cover lacks this boss and if fitted to a vehicle with a Series II or IIA gearbox, the clutch is unlikely to disengage properly.

To replace the clutch, the engine and gearbox must be separated. This requires one or the other to be removed, and there is normally little to choose between the two. On most Series vehicles, the gearbox must be lifted out from inside the vehicle, after removing the floors, transmission tunnel and seat box. Most ex-military vehicles have a detachable crossmember under the gearbox, which allows the transmission unit to be dropped out from underneath the vehicle. On a 109 V8, the transmission must come out from underneath, as the bellhousing is too long to be able to remove the unit from above. Without access to a vehicle lift and transmission jack it is difficult and possibly dangerous to try to remove the transmission from below, especially the LT95, which is very long and very, very heavy. So, on a 109 V8, it will normally make sense to remove the engine rather than the transmission, if the clutch requires replacement.

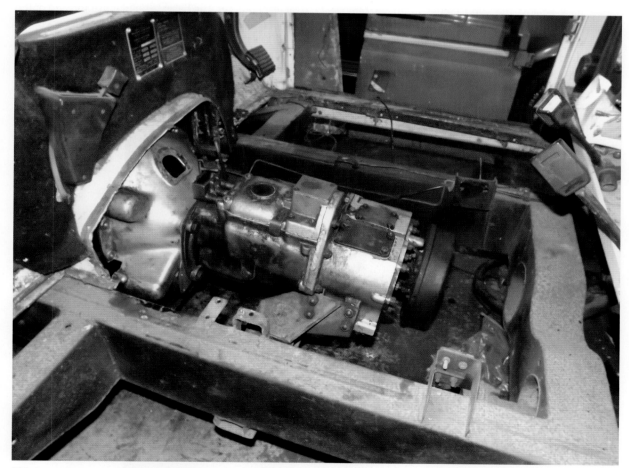

With the seat box removed, access to the transmission unit is straightforward.

The detachable gearbox crossmember is normally only found on military vehicles and 109 V8s.

The 4- and 6-cylinder transmissions can be removed fairly easily through the passenger side door using an engine hoist. You will find it much easier if you first unbolt the handbrake-operating crank from the chassis, and either detach the door check rod, so the passenger door can be folded back against the wing (Series II/IIA), or remove the door altogether (Series III). The brackets between the gearbox mounting rubbers and the chassis should be unbolted from the chassis, so that they come out with the gearbox. On Series II and IIA vehicles with the round

Smiths type heater, the heater unit should be removed to avoid the possibility of damaging it while manoeuvring the gearbox out of the vehicle. The gearbox can be supported for lifting by wrapping one end of a chain around the rear output housing and securing the other end to the gear lever bracket. The balance point is just forward of the join between the gearbox and transfer box. The back of the engine will need to be supported on a long jack, and carefully lifted as the gearbox is raised off its mounts.

The clutch is attached to the flywheel with six bolts,

Aligning the clutch plate using an old gearbox input shaft.

which should be loosened progressively, one turn at a time until all are loose. When removing the last bolt, make sure you support the clutch cover with one hand, so that it does not fall onto your foot – Land Rover clutch covers are surprisingly heavy. As with brakes, be aware that the clutch plate may (if very old) have asbestos linings, and the entire clutch, flywheel and gearbox bellhousing will be contaminated with asbestos dust. This should be washed away with water, and absolutely not blown off with an airline. With the clutch removed, inspect the face of the flywheel for evidence of scoring, cracks or other damage. A scored flywheel can usually be refaced by a machine shop. Check the condition of the spigot bush in the centre of the flywheel: this is a plain phosphor-bronze bush that supports the front of the gearbox input shaft. It should be replaced if worn, cracked or loose in its housing. Phosphor-bronze is brittle and the bush can easily be split with a sharp chisel (taking great care not to mark the housing) and extracted in pieces. A new bush should be soaked in clean engine oil for at least twenty-four hours before fitting, and when drifting it in, great care must be taken not to damage it, and especially not to flatten over the end, otherwise the gearbox shaft will not go into it.

When fitting the new clutch, the plate must be aligned so that it is exactly central on the flywheel before the cover bolts are tightened. An experienced mechanic can do this by eye, but it is much safer to use a clutch alignment tool. 'Universal' alignment tools, especially the cheap ones made of plastic, are often too inaccurate to do the job, and the same goes for the old trick of taking a length of wooden dowel and wrapping sticky tape around it. If the clutch plate is not correctly aligned, it will be impossible to mate the gearbox to the engine, so you really need to either buy or borrow a good-quality metal alignment tool or (even better) acquire an old input shaft from a scrap Series gearbox. With the clutch plate centred on the flywheel, the cover should be bolted loosely in place, and then the bolts tightened progressively, again one turn at a time. Be sure to fit new spring washers under the bolt heads, and once the cover bolts are fully tight, check that your clutch alignment tool is free to slide in and out without catching on the edge of the spigot bush.

Before bolting everything back together, you will need to check the condition of the clutch release mechanism. On Series II and IIA gearboxes, ensure that the clutch sleeve spins freely in the housing without any roughness, and give the moving surfaces a light smear of grease. Check the two pins in the cross-shaft between the clutch release housing and the bracket that holds the clutch slave cylinder and bellcrank: these pins often wear or shear. On the Series III, remove and discard the old clutch release bearing, remove the release fork and lubricate the pivot point and the end of the pushrod with grease. There is a plastic cup pressed into the clutch fork to bear on the pivot: make sure this is not missing before refitting the fork. Give the plain end and splines of the gearbox input shaft a light smear of grease. And on both types of gearbox, pull back the rubber dust cover on the clutch slave cylinder to check for fluid leaks, and replace, if the inside of the dust cover is wet with fluid.

Series III clutch master cylinder with integral reservoir.

As with engine refitting (*see* Chapter 8) the engine and gearbox must be brought together absolutely square in all planes, otherwise the gearbox input shaft will not slide cleanly through the clutch plate and into the spigot bush. If the engine and gearbox will not go back together, do not try to force them but try to work out why they will not fit. Either the angle is wrong (gearbox hanging incorrectly on the crane) or the clutch plate is not perfectly centralized on the flywheel. Once the two are together, tighten all the bellhousing nuts, then fit the bolts through the gearbox to chassis brackets before finally taking the weight of the gearbox off the crane. The brackets tend to be forced outwards under the weight of the gearbox, and you may need to lever them with a stout screwdriver to be able to push the bolts into place.

CLUTCH OPERATING SYSTEM

On all Series II, IIA and III Land Rovers, the clutch is operated by a hydraulic system consisting of a master cylinder (attached to the clutch pedal box and operated via a threaded adjustable pushrod), slave cylinder (attached to the gearbox via a bracket on Series II and IIA, bolted direct to the gearbox bellhousing on Series III) and a mechanism to transfer movement from the clutch slave cylinder to the clutch pressure plate (cross-shaft and bellcrank on Series II/IIA; a simple pivoting fork on Series III). The system is self-adjusting and once properly set up, should not require any adjustment or maintenance apart from periodic lubrication of the pivot points on the Series II/IIA cross-shaft.

Usual problems are: failure of the seals in the master cylinder (clutch pedal goes to the floor with no resistance when depressed slowly, fluid running down the clutch pedal), slave cylinder seal failure (system losing fluid) and (especially on Series II and IIA) internal collapse of the flexible hose between master and slave (clutch pedal stiff, clutch slow to engage). On the Series II and IIA, the cross-shaft goes into the side of the bellhousing, where it is connected to the clutch release mechanism with a sleeve and two steel pins. These can break, resulting in a clutch pedal that will not go all the way to the floor and difficulty in engaging gears. Problems with gear engagement can also be caused by air in the system.

On all vehicles it is important that the clutch master cylinder and pedal box are set up correctly. There are two adjustments: pedal height (measured from the floor, and adjusted via a bolt and locknut on the front face of the pedal box) and the free play on the master cylinder pushrod. It is absolutely vital that, with the pedal at the top of its travel, there should be a small amount of up and down movement in the pedal before the master cylinder starts to operate. If this is not present, the clutch hydraulics will tend to 'pump up' with repeated use, preventing the clutch from engaging fully and resulting in clutch slip.

The master cylinder is most easily replaced with the pedal box removed from the vehicle. Six bolts attach it to the footwell. It is just about possible to replace the master cylinder without removing the pedal box, but the lower of the two nuts and bolts securing the cylinder to the pedal box is tucked up right inside the pedal box and very hard to access. The new master cylinder should be fitted with a nut (5⁄16in UNF) and plain washer either side of the clevis through which the pushrod passes, and these nuts should be left loose until the pedal box has been refitted. While the pedal box is off the vehicle, it is a good idea to remove the blanking plug on the end of the pedal pivot and trickle some oil into the hole. The pedal should move freely throughout its travel with no stickiness or tight spots. The clevis should also be lubricated at each end.

With the pedal box in place, the pedal height should first be set to the specification in the workshop manual, then the pushrod free-play adjusted via the two nuts until there is just a small amount of slack at the very top of the pedal travel, then tightened against each other while holding the pushrod stationary with Mole grips or similar. This can be tricky, as access is limited: an old 1⁄2in (13mm) spanner with a slot cut in it to pass over the pushrod will be very helpful. Once you are happy that the master cylinder is correctly set up, it can be refilled with fresh fluid and the system bled.

Slave-cylinder replacement is not especially difficult, although access to the two mounting bolts and nuts on earlier vehicles can be tricky, especially early vehicles where the clutch slave cylinder is bolted to the bracket from underneath. You may need to detach the entire bracket and cross-shaft from the gearbox to gain access. Later Series IIAs have the slave cylinder bolted on from above. On the Series III, the mounting bolts screw directly into the aluminium bellhousing and have a nasty habit of stripping the thread when tightened. If this happens, you can try a slightly longer bolt (M8 metric) but if this does not work, you may have to fit Helicoil thread inserts. This is just about possible with the gearbox in the vehicle, after removing the exhaust downpipe. When fitting the new slave cylinder, note which way it goes – bleed nipple towards the rear of the vehicle on Series II and IIA, and towards the top of the slave cylinder on Series III.

GEARBOX OVERHAUL

As noted above, the overhaul of a Series II, IIA or III gearbox is not especially difficult, although to change the bearings you will ideally need a hydraulic press. Simply by following the instructions in the workshop manual, any moderately competent home-mechanic should end up with a gearbox that performs as well as it did when it left the factory. However, there are a few specific issues on the 4- and 6-cylinder gearboxes that require particularly close attention:

Transfer box internals are massively strong and seldom fail.

◆ **Pinion and layshaft gear (the two gears at the very front of the gearbox):** these are a matched pair and must be replaced as such. Mixing and matching between gear sets will give you a gearbox that howls in every gear except top.

◆ **Layshaft securing nut (bolt on Series III):** this must be tightened to the correct torque, and secured with a new split pin (II/IIA) or Loctited (III). A loose layshaft nut on a Series II/IIA gearbox will result in a broken layshaft. A loose bolt on a Series III gearbox will wreck the gearbox casing.

◆ **Mainshaft snap ring:** this is buried deep inside the centre of third gear and inaccessible with almost any snap ring pliers you can buy. The trick is to take half a dozen lengths of steel rod, grind the ends to a taper and then drive them down the inside of the snap ring to force it clear of the splines. The mainshaft can then be pressed through the centre of third gear, taking the snap ring with it. Always replace the snap ring with a new one.

◆ **Third/fourth synchromesh hub:** this can easily be fitted the wrong way round. If you look closely at the central part, one end has a recess machined in it. This is to clear the snap ring mentioned above, and now that you understand this, you will not fit the hub incorrectly.

◆ **Reverse gear idler (Series III Suffix B onwards, roller bearing type):** beware of non-genuine replacements, as they are often machined incorrectly. They look fine but will cause the gearbox to jump violently out of reverse gear under load. A Series transmission specialist should be aware of this issue and will be able to supply a modified gear.

◆ **Design modifications:** many components within these gearboxes were redesigned over the years and the changes are often subtle and hard to detect from visual inspection. Before ordering new parts, make sure you know exactly what kind of gearbox you have: this can normally be determined from the serial number. Do not discard old, worn components without first comparing them to the new replacements you have bought. Measure the diameter and count the gear teeth. Just because a replacement component appears to physically fit, it does not follow that it will work correctly.

The gearbox rear mainshaft nut is castellated and you need a special tool to undo it. This one was made using an old socket and an angle grinder.

Serial number location on Series II, IIA and early Series III transmissions.

Serial number on later Series III transmissions is stamped on the transfer box.

A Rover differential removed from the axle casing.

axles, hubs and propshafts

All these vehicles have big, strong beam axles, front and rear, which have played a big part in making Land Rover's reputation for durability and off-road performance. There are two types you are likely to find: the 'Rover' axle, carried over, front and rear, from the Series One; and the heavy-duty 'Salisbury' axle, fitted to the rear of the Series III 109in and sometimes retrofitted to earlier vehicles.

The basic front axle design, common to almost all Series vehicles, consists of a strong pressed-steel axle case, with chrome swivel balls bolted to flanges welded to each end. Cast swivel housings pivot on an upper bush and lower roller bearing pressed into the swivel ball, with the brake backplate and stub axle bolted to the outer face of the swivel housing. The housing itself is filled with oil, with a large, circular rubber seal between the swivel housing and the chrome ball, which (at least in theory) keeps the oil where it should be. The differential is self-contained within a substantial cast housing and secured to the casing with a ring of nuts and studs. Halfshafts have ten splines on the inner end, and either ten or twenty-four on the outer, depending on model and year. They are fully floating, with

the outer end being retained in position by the drive flange and a bearing in the centre of the chrome ball to support the joint. Some later axles have a plain bush at the inner end of the stub axle to provide additional support. The inner and outer ends of each halfshaft are connected by a Hardy–Spicer universal joint, lubricated by the oil in the swivel housing.

Front half-shafts: the twenty-four-spline-type is visibly stronger than the ten-spline.

On early Series IIs (up to 1960), the upper swivel bush consisted of a tapered, spring-loaded cone bearing on a brass seat, with the steering arm splined into the cone and mounted on the top of the swivel housing. This proved unsatisfactory – the splines on the steering arm tended to wear, leading to an alarming steering shimmy at speed. So the 'cup and cone' setup was replaced with a plain, large-diameter steel pin inside a composite-lined steel 'Railko' bush, and at the same time, the steering arms were moved to the bottom of the swivel housing.

Around 1967, the differential stud design was changed. Earlier axles had BSF bolts screwed through the casing from the inside and lockwired in place. The lockwires tended to break, making it impossible to undo the nuts, so the bolts were replaced with flat-headed splined ⅜in UNF studs, which seldom give any problems. For the launch of the Series III in 1971, long-wheelbase models received stronger halfshafts with twenty-four-spline outer ends and drive flanges. The hubs were given stronger M16 splined wheel studs to replace the smaller threaded and peined type. In July 1980, the stronger twenty-four-spline axle was adopted for short-wheelbase vehicles. Three months later, the stub axle was redesigned to incorporate an internal plain bush. At the same time, the hubs were redesigned and now had equal-sized inner and outer bearings, and a new design of inner seal.

For the launch of the 109 V8 ('Stage One') in 1979, the axle design was substantially modified. The spring mounts on the axle casing were relocated to tilt the nose of the differential upwards, and the halfshafts were fitted with constant velocity joints to cope with the demands of permanent four-wheel drive. This necessitated enlarging the inside of the swivel housings and redesigning the upper and lower swivel pins to provide additional clearance. The differential was changed to 3.54:1 ratio, identical to that used in the Range Rover at the time. Parts for these Stage One axles are now very hard indeed to obtain.

Finally, a very small number of Series IIIs (mostly One Ton models and armoured car conversions) were fitted with heavy-duty 'Salisbury' front axles. These have the chrome swivels welded to the axle casing. It is unlikely that you will come across one, but be warned that if the swivels are rusted, having them re-plated will not be cheap.

1958–60 swivel assembly with top-mounted 'pendant' arm.

Later swivel assembly with bottom-mounted arm.

Pre-1980 (left) and post-1980 Series III hubs showing the different seal designs. All Series III hubs have massively strong pull-through wheel studs.

This 1965 Series IIA 109in has acquired the stronger Salisbury rear axle from a Series III.

All short-wheelbase vehicles, and long-wheelbase Series II and IIA, share the same rear-axle design, with a pressed-steel case and differential similar to that at the front. The halfshafts and drive flanges are 'fully floating' with the same hub and wheel-bearing design as at the front, and have ten splines on the halfshafts at both inner and outer ends. The design was arguably not quite strong enough for the heavier loads of long-wheelbase models and gained a reputation for breaking halfshafts. As an interim measure, Land Rover introduced a stronger rear axle as an option, bought in from ENV. These were never common and parts availability is poor.

For the launch of the Series III, a heavy-duty 'Salisbury' rear axle was standardized for long-wheelbase models. This is a heavy but impressively robust unit that seldom gives problems. Apart from the hub design being changed at the same time as the front in 1980 (with new stub axles to suit), the Salisbury axle remained standard on long-wheelbase Series IIIs through to the end of production. The 109 V8 had a 3.54:1 ratio version of the same axle.

HUBS

All these vehicles share the same basic design, with a pair of taper roller bearings running on a strong, hollow stub axle bolted to the axle case, and a seal between the hub and the inner end of the stub axle. The bearings are substantial and, if properly maintained, will last almost indefinitely. Problems are usually caused by lack of lubrication, especially at the front where they rely on the oil inside the swivel housing and can be destroyed when the swivel seal fails and allows the oil to escape. Hub seals are a frequent source

of problems, especially on pre-1980 vehicles. The threaded wheel studs on pre-1971 hubs have a habit of rusting to the wheel nuts and coming out of the hub when the nuts are undone. This usually chews up the thread in the hub. Series III (and very late Series IIA) hubs have much stronger pull-through splined studs and do not suffer from this problem.

A failed hub seal is easy to spot: with the brake drum removed, you will see that the brake backplate and the body of the hub are wet with oil. Replacement is a simple matter of removing the old seal (with a hook-type seal puller) and pressing in a new one. Until the mid-1970s, Land Rover fitted metal-cased seals with a leather insert, which are still available; they need to be soaked in clean oil for at least twenty-four hours before fitting. For this reason alone, most people prefer the later rubber seal. Note that there are two different types. Pre-1980 vehicles have hubs with unequal-sized inner and outer bearings. These use seal RTC3510, which should be carefully pressed in so that the outer face is flush with the end of the hub. For later vehicles with equal-sized inner and outer bearings, the seal is RTC3511 and should be pressed in until it contacts the lip on the inside of the hub. These later seals are far more reliable than the earlier ones but cannot be fitted to pre-1980 hubs; nor can the later hub be fitted to a pre-1980 stub axle.

Before refitting the hub it is important to ascertain why the old seal failed. There are four possibilities: sheer old age (the seal will be hard and inflexible), incorrect fitting (especially on pre-1980 hubs where there is no lip to stop the seal being pressed in too far or out of square), a scored stub axle or a blocked axle breather. Inspect the stub axle carefully, especially at the inner end where the seal bears against it (the area known as the 'land'). This surface should

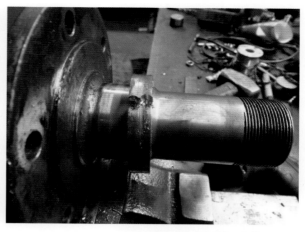

TOP LEFT: Badly rusted and scored land will quickly destroy a new hub seal.

TOP RIGHT: Chain-drill the land to weaken it, ensuring you do not drill into the stub axle itself.

RIGHT: After chain-drilling, the land is split with a sharp chisel.

be clean and smooth, without scoring or corrosion. Minor surface rust can be cleaned up with fine-grade wet and dry paper, but any significant imperfections in the surface will rapidly chew up the new seal. On pre-1980 stub axles, the land can be replaced by drilling several small holes through it to weaken it (being careful not to drill through into the stub axle), splitting it with a sharp chisel and pressing on a new one. Post-1980 stub axles do not have a removable land: minor damage can be machined out on a lathe, but if this is not possible the entire stub axle will need to be replaced.

Axle breathers are the small brass valves that screw into the top of each axle casing. Each contains a small ball bearing. When the axle gets hot, the air in it expands: the breather prevents pressure from building up and forcing oil past the seals. The ball bearing often rusts and sticks. The breather cannot easily be dismantled, and it is better to simply replace it with a new one (part number 515845).

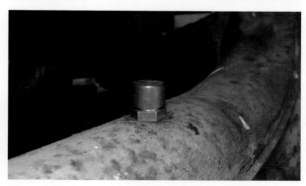

The breather screws into the top of the axle casing and should be checked if a hub seal has failed.

A failed wheel bearing will be felt as rumbling and roughness when the wheel is rotated. The bearing assemblies consist of two parts: the bearing itself and the outer steel 'race', which is pressed into the hub. Bearings and races come as matched assemblies and should never be mixed; nor should a new bearing be fitted to an old race. If a bearing is suspect, it should be removed, cleaned and carefully inspected. Any scoring or pitting on the rollers or race means that it is scrap. The race can be removed by drifting it out from inside the hub with a sharp chisel, working around the circumference a couple of taps at a time. There is only a very small protruding edge to tap. Do not discard the old race; instead cut a slot through it crossways with a disc cutter. Thoroughly clean up the recess in the hub, place the new race in position and use the old race on top as a tubular drift, tapping on alternate sides to keep the new race square as it goes in. Once it is fully home, the slot in the old race allows it to be easily removed.

This bearing race has chunks of metal missing from it. Not much doubt here about the need for replacement.

Drift the bearing race out of the hub with a good chisel.

An old outer bearing race slotted to use as a drift.

Tapping in the new bearing race, using the old one.

New bearings should normally just be given a light smear of bearing grease, as they will be lubricated by the axle oil. Late Series IIIs (with equal-sized inner and outer bearings) have a seal inside the front axle that prevents the oil in the swivel housing from reaching the bearings. Some earlier vehicles will have semi-fluid grease rather than oil in the swivel housings. If this is the case, the bearings must be packed with grease before fitting. Make sure your hands are thoroughly clean, take the bearing in one hand and a big dollop of grease in the other, and press the grease into the bearing, squeezing it between the rollers. Drop the inner bearing into the hub, fit the seal, then fit the outer bearing before locating the assembly on the stub axle.

The hub is secured to the stub axle by a pair of large nuts with a locking tab in between them. To undo the nuts, you

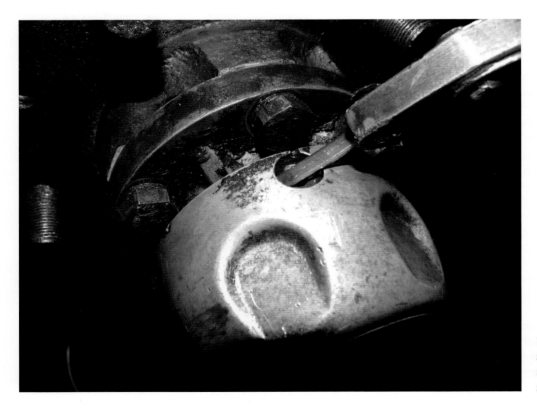

To dismantle Fairey free-wheeling hubs, this plastic tab must first be extracted.

will need the appropriate box spanner or deep socket (2¹⁄₁₆in/52mm). You will almost certainly find that a previous owner has removed the outer nut (and possibly the inner) with a hammer and chisel. This is a bad idea as bits can break off the damaged nut and find their way into the bearing, which is not good for the rollers. Damaged nuts should be replaced (part number FRC8700). With the hub located on the stub axle, fit the thick tab washer, then the inner nut. Tighten this while revolving the hub until it just starts to drag, then back it off a fraction so that the hub spins freely. Fit a new locking tab (part number 217353, costs pennies – don't you dare try to reuse the old one!) and tighten the outer nut. Then check the hub still spins freely. You may well find that tightening the outer nut pushes the inner nut against the threads and causes the hub to bind – in this case, remove the outer nut and tab, slacken the inner nut just a fraction, then try again. The hub should turn freely, but without any looseness or rattling from the bearings. Once you are happy, bend one side of the locktab against the flat of the inner nut (using a blunt chisel) and the opposite side against the outer nut.

Damaged hub studs are quite common on Series II and IIA hubs. If the thread is intact, a new stud can be screwed in and the inner end peined over with a hammer and drift to secure it. If (as is usually the case) the thread is damaged, the hole will need to be drilled out absolutely square to ⁹⁄₁₆in and a repair stud fitted (561886). This is a flat-headed splined stud and should be either pressed in or (if you do not have a press) drawn through the hub using a good undamaged wheel nut and a thick spacing washer. Pre-1980 Series III hubs are fully interchangeable with the earlier type, have thicker, stronger studs and larger wheel nuts, and are well worth fitting, if you can obtain them, especially on vehicles that have oversized tyres or are used extensively off-road.

DIFFERENTIAL AND HALFSHAFTS

Differential failure on these vehicles is relatively uncommon and usually caused by heavy off-road use or being run very low on oil. A worn differential will 'howl' at speed. The Rover differential is a self-contained unit and easy

A 'typical' hub nut – attacked with a chisel. At least the locking tab does not appear to have been reused.

Hub nut tools: deep socket, box spanner and the cold chisel that far too many people use instead. A chisel is not a spanner.

Series II/IIA hub, showing inadequate method of retaining the original studs, and a pull-through repair stud.

to replace after withdrawing the halfshafts and undoing the ring of bolts that hold it to the axle casing. Although theoretically repairable, differentials require very careful measurement and setting up after overhaul; you will probably find it much easier to replace a faulty differential with a good second-hand unit. The rear axle case on most of these vehicles does not have a filler/level plug on it, so if replacing a rear differential, you will need the type that has a filler plug incorporated in the body. Be sure to check the ratio: Series' differentials are 4.7:1, and look almost identical to the 3.54:1 unit on later Land Rovers and the much rarer 4.11:1 units more usually found in Rover P5 saloon cars. Mark the edge of the crown wheel with a dab of white paint or Tippex, then count the number of turns of the drive flange required for one complete revolution of the crown wheel. Just over four and a half is what you are looking for. Of course, this assumes that your vehicle has not been fitted with 3.54:1 differentials by a previous owner, so check the ratio of the old differential as well as the new one.

The Salisbury differential is a completely different beast and can only be replaced using a special spreader tool that stretches the axle casing. It is most unlikely that you will be able to get your hands on one of these, so a failed Salisbury axle is best replaced as a complete unit. The good news is that the Salisbury axle very, very rarely gives problems, apart from the tapered filler plug that screws into the pressed steel rear differential cover: it is easy to overtighten this and distort the cover, so that the threaded plug no longer seals properly. A loose plug can actually vibrate itself inwards and drop inside the axle casing where it causes mechanical carnage, so do not ignore this fault. The only solution is to replace the cover. Fortunately this is fairly easy, as it just bolts onto the axle casing.

Oil leaking past the pinion seal (behind the flange where the propshaft attaches) is very common. If the leak is minor, the first step is to check the axle breather: replacing a blocked breather will often cure the leak. On the Rover axle, replacing a seal is fairly easy once you have removed the drive flange, which is retained with a castellated nut and split pin that can be hard to extract. The nut is done up very tight; you may need to buy, borrow or make a tool to hold the flange steady, so that you can use a big breaker bar on the nut. Earlier differentials have a seal carrier retained by a ring of six bolts; on later ones the seal is pressed direct into the casing. If the seal is the rubber type, it can be extracted with a hook-type puller and a new seal tapped into place until it seats on the lip inside the housing. Many earlier differentials still have the old steel and leather seals, which are best dealt with by removing the seal carrier and drifting out the seal with a large punch. The part number for a new seal is FRC4586, and do not forget to fit a new split pin once you have tightened the flange nut. Also, be sure to check the drive flange for scoring and corrosion because if badly damaged, it will wreck the new seal.

Replacing the seal on a Salisbury differential is trickier. The drive flange nut is a Nyloc and probably very tight indeed. As well as securing the drive flange, it is also used to set the pinion-bearing preload by means of a collapsible spacer. On refitting the drive flange, if the nut is tightened any further on the thread than when it was removed, this may cause the pinion bearing to lock up solid. And just to add to the fun, the seal itself is a metal and leather item; the old one will probably be a pig to remove, and the replacement will need soaking in oil for at least a day before fitting. An upgraded metal and rubber seal was fitted to the Defender 110 and will fit the Series Salisbury axle, but is quite expensive compared to the standard seal.

Front halfshafts seldom give problems unless the swivel housings are run dry of oil or the vehicle has been used extensively off-road. They consist of an inner and outer shaft with a conventional Hardy–Spicer joint between the two halves. To remove a front halfshaft, the hub, brake backplate and stub axle need to come off. Provided the splines on each end are in good condition, the joint can then be replaced in the same way as a propshaft joint. The 109 V8 has a completely different design with a constant velocity joint, and being permanent four-wheel drive, the front halfshafts are far more likely to suffer from worn splines than on other Series' vehicles. A worn CV joint will make a loud clicking noise with the steering on full lock. Parts for these axles are now very hard indeed to obtain.

Rear halfshafts on the Rover axle can break, usually at the inner end, leading to total loss of drive. If this happens, selecting four-wheel drive will get you home. This type of failure usually requires removal of both halfshafts and the differential, so that the broken stub of the halfshaft can be extracted. Persistent breakage of the outer end of the halfshaft is much rarer and usually the result of a bent stub axle. The splined ends wear, as do the drive flanges, leading to a noticeable 'clonk' when taking up drive. Salisbury halfshafts are very much stronger, but sadly not interchangeable with the Rover type. They can suffer from worn splines at the outer end (and in the drive flange).

AXLE CASINGS

Corrosion or impact damage to the axle casing itself is not unknown, especially with some of these vehicles now being nearly sixty years old. Corrosion usually affects the large, round differential pan on Rover axles, and the strengthening box section that runs along the bottom of the casing on most Rover rear axles. Replacement pans are available but need to be very carefully welded in to avoid oil leaks. The box section is not currently available as a ready-made repair section but can be fabricated from 4mm steel sheet. Small corrosion pinholes and cracks from impact damage in the pan can be repaired with an epoxy-based product, such as Leak-Fix, but it is essential that the oil is drained and the area around the hole is thoroughly cleaned back to dry, bare metal, if the repair is to hold. Larger cracks can be either welded or (preferably) brazed.

SWIVEL HOUSINGS

The chrome swivel ball deteriorates with age: the chrome plating becomes damaged, starts to flake off and rust takes hold. The rough surface rapidly wears away the large, round seal between swivel housing and ball, resulting in oil all over the inside edge of the tyre. Even with the swivel ball in good condition, the seal wears and hardens with age. If

A freshly rebuilt swivel assembly, hopefully good for very many years to come.

the pitting is not too bad, it is often possible to prolong its life by rubbing down the corroded areas, treating them with a rust converter, which turns the rust into a hard black substance, then sanding this smooth and fitting a new seal. To replace the seal, the complete swivel assembly must be removed from the front axle: it is attached with six BSF nuts and bolts, which should be renewed on reassembly. An alternative 'quick fix' is to drain the oil out of the swivel housing (if it still contains any) and fill it with semi-fluid grease (STC3435). If this is done, the hub bearings will have to be stripped, cleaned and packed with bearing grease, as they will no longer be properly lubricated.

The swivel housing can also become loose on the ball due to wear in the upper pin and lower bearing, and compression of the fibre thrust washer under the upper pin (on post-1960 vehicles). Check for movement between the housing and ball by 'rocking' the wheel while an assistant stands on the brake pedal. If you can still feel movement with the brakes applied, there is excess play in the swivel. This can often be taken out by removing a couple of shims from under the top swivel pin, or replacing the fibre thrust washer. When adjusting swivel preload in this way, the track rod and drag link should be disconnected from the steering arms. If you remove too many shims, the steering will be very stiff and heavy.

Eventually the entire assembly becomes too corroded and/or worn for further service and will need to be rebuilt. The upper pin can wear badly on vehicles that have been

run with the swivel housings dry of oil. On 1958–60 'cup and cone' swivels, the splines on the steering arm wear and lead to inconsistent preload and steering wobble. The lower swivel bearing can break up, again due to lack of oil, giving a heavy and notchy feel to the steering. Replacing a swivel ball is quite a long job but not beyond the abilities of a good home-mechanic armed with a workshop manual. The main points to watch are:

◆ The swivel housing is asymmetric. There is a plain bush at the top and a roller bearing at the bottom, which you will have to press in yourself, using a hydraulic press. Make sure you get them the right way round, using the old swivel housing for reference.

◆ A kit is available to convert the 'cup and cone' upper pin to the more reliable Railko system. This includes plain pins to replace the splined pins in the steering arms. The part number for this kit is 532268.

◆ It is quite likely that some or all of the studs for the steering arms will come out with the nuts. These must be refitted securely before the arms go back on.

◆ Note that two of the studs for each steering arm have a larger diameter than the other two. There need to be two large-diameter studs fitted to each housing; otherwise the steering arms will work loose.

◆ Bearing preload should be set up as per the manual, using a spring balance (fishing scales do the job nicely) and before fitting the large swivel seal.

Chrome swivels are asymmetric and the correct bearing must be fitted to each end.

◆ The recess for the swivel seal needs to be thoroughly clean, smooth and free of corrosion. A thin bead of RTV sealant around the edge of the seal will help to keep the assembly oiltight.

◆ Locking tabs are fitted to the swivel pin and steering arm nuts/bolts and the stub axle bolts, except on post-1980 axles, where the stub axle bolts are retained with Loctite. As always, locking tabs must always be renewed on reassembly.

PROPSHAFTS

On most Series vehicles these are of very conventional design with a four-bolt drive flange and Hardy–Spicer joint at each end, and a sliding spline in between. The exception is the 109 V8 front propshaft, which has a double Hardy–Spicer joint with centralizing device at the gearbox end to compensate for the differential pinion shaft not being parallel with the gearbox output. The joints are replaceable but the sliding spline is not. A small amount of rotational play at the splines is acceptable, but if the splines are so worn that the propshaft can be moved up and down, the entire assembly will require replacement. Propshafts can also become bent through over-enthusiastic off-road driving. A bent propshaft, or one with badly worn splines or a failed joint, will send a harsh vibration through the vehicle at higher speeds, which often changes or disappears when you back off the throttle.

To remove the propshaft, it will be helpful if you have the correct socket – a $^9\!/_{16}$in socket on a long, slim shaft. These are available from most Land Rover specialists. The nuts for the front end of the rear propshaft, in particular, are very hard to undo without this tool. When refitting the propshaft, always use new Nyloc nuts – $^3\!/_8$in UNF, apart from a handful of early Series IIs, which used BSF fasteners presumably left over from Series One production.

The quickest way to change a propshaft joint is to take a disc cutter to it, using a 1mm cutting disc. Cut through the

central 'spider' just below the end cup on each side, taking great care not to cut into the yoke itself. Once the spider has been removed, the cups can be drifted inwards with an old 12mm socket and the circlips prised out and discarded. This is a lot easier than trying to remove rusty circlips with the cups in place. Before fitting the new joint, the recesses for the cups should be thoroughly cleaned, along with the recesses for the circlips. Note that early Series II propshafts have a smaller joint than the others – $2^{15}\!/_{16}$in across the yokes, as opposed to $3^7\!/_{32}$in for the more common later type. Strangely, the early small joint is exactly the same as the one on most Defenders. Part numbers are RTC3458 for the early joint, RTC3346 for the later type.

Take the new joint and carefully withdraw two of the cups from opposing sides. Take the drive flange, grease the inside of the cup recesses and press on the cup into the flange until the inner edge is flush with the inner end of the recess. Make sure you press the cup in square or it will jam. Now smother the ends of the spider in grease, insert one end into the empty cup recess in the yoke, then carefully insert the other end into the cup. Throughout this process you need to be very, very careful not to dislodge the tiny needle rollers inside the cups. Locate the second cup and slowly squeeze the two cups together, ensuring that both ends of the spider seat correctly in the cups. Once the outer ends of the cups are flush with the yoke, use a large nut as a spacer to press one of them in further until the circlip can be fitted. Then use the spacer nut to press the other cup in until the second circlip will snap into place, making sure that both circlips are fully seated in the grooves. The flange and joint can then be attached to the main body of the propshaft using the same technique.

The double joint on the 109 V8 front propshaft is much trickier, not least because it has the circlips on the inside of the joints rather than the outside. To be honest, if you need to replace one of these joints you are probably best advised to take it to a propshaft specialist.

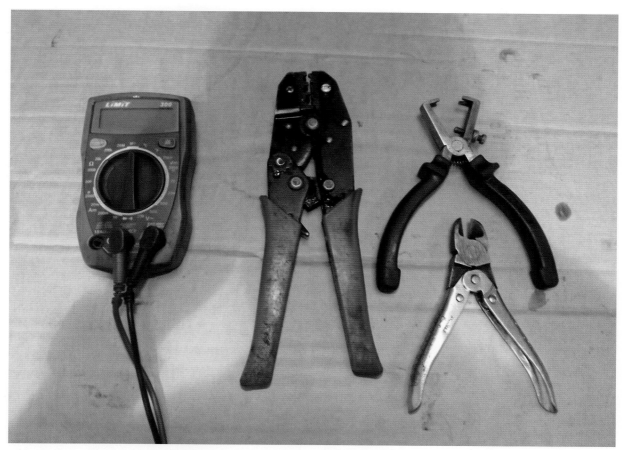

Basic electrical tools: multimeter, wire-cutters, wire-strippers and a decent terminal crimping tool.

11

electrical systems

Series II, IIA and III Land Rovers all have simple and conventional 12V systems using mostly off-the-shelf components shared with many other British vehicles of the same era. Over the years, the systems became progressively more complicated as new items were added to meet legis-lative changes and customer demands: the last Series IIIs had hazard flashers, rear fog-light, reversing light and two-speed windscreen wipers. On the first Series IIs, even the indicators and heater were optional extras. However, none of these vehicles are electrically complex: almost any electrical fault can be diagnosed using a multimeter, a wiring diagram and some common sense. The electrical system can broadly be broken down into three areas – starting, charging and body electrics (lights, wipers, gauges, etc.).

STARTING

The heart of a good starting system is the battery. Old Land Rovers have big, inefficient, power-hungry starter motors that need plenty of current, especially diesels. Series II and IIA diesels up to 1967 left the factory with two 6V batteries connected in series – one under the bonnet, the other beneath the passenger seat – but almost all of them will have been converted to a single 12V battery by now. The battery tray is generously dimensioned and will take a wide variety of different types but for almost all applications, a type 069 battery (as specified by Land Rover on the Series III diesel) will be more than adequate. Cheap batteries are cheap for a reason and tend to expire without warning shortly after the end of the warranty. Stick to a brand you have heard of. The battery should be firmly secured in the battery tray, ideally with the original battery clamp, which fits over the top and is secured with J bolts and wing nuts. If you are unlucky enough to roll your Land Rover onto its roof, you will already be in enough trouble without having the battery fall out, short on the underside of the bonnet and set fire to the wreckage.

Starter motors come in two flavours: inertia and pre-engaged. An inertia starter (4- and 6-cylinder petrol engines) has a sliding gear running in a spiral groove on the shaft, which is thrown into engagement with the flywheel when power is applied to the motor. On a pre-engaged starter (diesels and V8s), the drive gear is engaged by a solenoid attached to the motor, which applies current to the motor once the gear is fully engaged. Inertia starters tend to wear the teeth off the flywheel over time, so that

This battery is a little small for the job, but at least it is securely clamped in place.

Battery specifications: 600 CCA and 73AH are about the minimum you will need.

Standard Lucas diesel starter (top) and modern, compact Bosch replacement.

4-cylinder petrol starter motor.

Tractor-type key start on a 1960 Series II diesel.

Starter solenoid for 4- and 6-cylinder petrol vehicles, 1967 onwards.

the starter itself is defective. Note that the separate solenoid on petrol vehicles relies on a good, clean earth contact between the solenoid body and whatever it is bolted to.

If at the end of the process you have decided that the starter itself is faulty, replacement is not difficult. Remember to disconnect the battery before detaching the wiring from the starter motor. The starters on 4- and 6-cylinder petrol engines are interchangeable with each other but not with any other models. On the diesels, any 2.25 or 2.5 diesel starter will fit, from the big Lucas units on early Series IIs to the Bosch geared starter from a Discovery 300TDi, which is about half the size of the old Lucas unit yet more powerful. High-torque modern geared starters are available to replace the old-fashioned units on the petrol engines (including the V8); these are of the pre-engaged type and, on the 4- and 6-cylinder vehicles, you will need to fit and wire a separate solenoid to operate the starter.

CHARGING

Series II and IIA vehicles mostly left Solihull with a dynamo charging system. This consists of the dynamo itself, driven off the fan belt, and a separate control box mounted on the bulkhead. By the late 1960s, such systems had fallen out of favour. The standard Lucas C40 dynamo (as fitted to older Land Rovers) develops just 22A, which is barely

Original C40 dynamo fitted to a 2.25 diesel.

An alternator will keep the battery charged more effectively than a dynamo.

they no longer engage properly; pre-engaged types burn out the contacts on the solenoid instead. Whatever the type, the condition of the heavy cables that carry current from the battery to the starter is critical: dirty or loose connections are far more common than actual starter motor failures.

Petrol vehicles up to 1967 had the starter motor operated via a large push-button switch on the firewall; from 1967 onwards, starting was via a key switch that energized a heavy-duty solenoid, mounted either on the bulkhead (Series IIA) or the air-cleaner support (Series III). The push-button switches seem to last forever; the later solenoids are far less reliable. So you turn the key/press the button and nothing happens, or the starter turns over too slowly to fire up the engine: what then?

First check the battery. With everything switched off, put a multimeter across the terminals. A fully charged battery should give a reading of 12.8V or thereabouts; anything under 12.6V indicates that it is either flat or faulty. Try jump starting, substituting the battery with a known good one or taking it to a car accessory shop and asking them to test it. If the battery is fine, next check all the cable connectors from the battery terminals to the starter, including the earth strap that runs from the starter motor to the chassis, and the point where the battery earth cable bolts to the chassis.

Still nothing? Check the starter solenoid and ignition switch or push-button. On vehicles with a starter solenoid (whether separate or built in to the starter motor), when you turn the key you should hear a loud 'clonk' as the solenoid operates. If you cannot hear this, try feeding power direct from the battery to the small spade terminal on the solenoid (the one with the white and red wire going to it). If the starter now operates, the ignition switch or wiring is at fault. If not, or if the solenoid 'clonks' but does not activate the starter, then the solenoid itself is most likely to blame. If the starter operates very slowly and you are sure that the battery and all the connections are good, almost certainly

Voltmeter on a Series IIA with factory-fitted alternator charging – a rare sight.

enough to power lights, wipers and heater together, and at idle that output falls to zero. So, the Series III was fitted with a Lucas 16ACR alternator offering 34A and the ability to keep the battery charged, even with the engine idling and the headlights on. Alternator charging was offered as a factory option on late Series IIAs. These vehicles can easily be identified as they have a voltmeter in place of the charge warning light on the dashboard, but they are very rare indeed, even more so with the original 11AC alternator and separate regulator.

It is perfectly possible to convert a Series II or IIA to alternator charging using a Series III alternator and mounting bracket, and many vehicles have been thus converted. To remove the old dynamo mounting bracket, the front crankshaft pulley needs to come off, but on all but very early engines, the old bracket will not get in the way of the new one and can be left in place. The Series III cast mounting bracket and tensioner strap bolt straight onto the engine: the bracket is secured with two short bolts on the front and a much longer bolt passing through the engine block

Series IIA engine fitted with a Series III alternator bracket, with the old dynamo bracket left in place.

into a blind threaded hole in the back of the bracket. This is normally threaded 5/16in UNF but some late brackets are M8 metric. Wiring is a little more complex. There are two wires going to the dynamo: one with a large spade terminal and the other small. These plug straight into the back of the alternator; there are two large spade connectors on the alternator, but either will do. Although only designed for 22A, the dynamo wiring will just about handle the 34A output of a standard Series alternator, if in perfect condition; but if there is any doubt, the thicker of the two cables should be replaced with one that is rated to carry at least 34A.

The control box on the bulkhead will need to be bypassed – whether you remove it altogether is up to you. There are five terminals marked A1, A, F, D and E. Disconnect all of them, marking them with tape as you go. Wires A1, A and F should be connected to each other, either with solder (and properly insulated after joining) or using a heavy-duty insulated screw terminal. The two wires from D should be connected to each other: this completes the circuit for the charge warning light. Some late vehicles have a different control box: on these connect D to WL and F to B. In both cases, E is the earth wire for the control box and does not need to be connected to anything.

If you choose to retain the dynamo charging system (and for reasons of originality, some people do), it has the advantage that faults in the system can be quite easily diagnosed and often repaired, whereas the solid-state regulator inside a 16ACR alternator either works or not. Whether dynamo or alternator, if a charging fault is suspected, the first step is to get out the multimeter and check the voltage at the battery. With the engine held at a speed well above idle, you should be seeing something around 13.5V, and this should not drop significantly when the headlights are switched on. Below 13V and the system is not generating enough power to keep the battery charged. Anything above 14.5V indicates a regulator fault and will fairly quickly boil the battery dry. And if, on a dynamo-equipped vehicle, the charge warning light stays on after you switch the engine off, disconnect the battery immediately – the regulator has stuck, turning the dynamo into an electric motor, which is now trying to turn the engine over.

BODY ELECTRICS

Most body electrical faults are caused by bad connections. Land Rover made extensive use of male bullet connectors joined with rubber-cased metal joiners, which are thinly plated steel and corrode, especially the ones behind the radiator grille for the headlight wiring. To diagnose electrical faults, you will need to be able to read a wiring diagram. All the wires in the loom are colour-coded, being either a single colour or a main colour with a thinner stripe (or 'trace') of a different colour running along them. The wiring colours remained unchanged throughout Series II, IIA and III production and, once you become familiar with them, you will be able to do a great deal without even having to look at the diagram. The main colours used are shown in the table.

Main wiring colours

Main colour	Trace colour	Function
Brown	–	Feed direct from battery – unfused
Purple	–	Feed direct from battery – fused
White	–	Feed via ignition switch – unfused
Green	–	Feed via ignition switch – fused
Green	Red	Indicator circuit – left side
Green	White	Indicator circuit – right side
Blue	–	Headlamps – before dip switch
Blue	Red	Headlamps – dip beam
Blue	White	Headlamps – main beam
Red	–	Sidelights front
Red	Black	Tail lights rear
Red	Yellow	Fog-light rear
Red	White	Instrument panel lights
Green	Purple	Brake lights
Green	Brown	Reversing lights
Green	Black	Fuel gauge to tank sender
Green	Blue	Temperature gauge to sender
Green	Yellow	Oil pressure light to switch
White	Red	Starter switch to solenoid
White	Black	Ignition coil to distributor
Brown	Yellow	Charge warning light to alternator
Brown	Black	Horn switch to horn
Purple	White	Dash switch to interior light
Black	–	Earth

The cause of most electrical faults will quickly become obvious provided you adopt a methodical approach, but there are a few that are slightly more unusual. Here are some that you might come across, whose cause may not be immediately obvious:

◆ **High-temperature and fuel-gauge readings (Series IIA 1967 onwards, Series III):** the fuel and temperature gauges are powered via a voltage stabilizer, which limits the supply to 10V. The stabilizer is a small tin box, either screwed to the bulkhead behind the instrument panel (Series IIA) or attached to the back of the speedometer (Series III). It often fails either because of a bad earth or corrosion where the tin cover is crimped over one of the contacts. Part number is 148876. On a Series III, if the gauges read high and the speedometer does not illuminate, the fault is most likely in the earth connection to the speedometer body (black wire, ring terminal, clamped under one of the speedometer securing nuts).

◆ **Fuel gauge always reads full (Series II/IIA 1958–67):** bad connection somewhere between the fuel gauge and the sender unit on the tank. Early fuel gauges work on a different principle to later ones, and if the sender is not connected, they will read full rather than empty.

◆ **Fuel gauge works backwards (Series II/IIA 1958–67):** late-type tank sender fitted in place of the early type. This is quite common: early senders are expensive; later ones cheap. The early sender has a square box on top with two nut terminals. Late type has a flat top with spade terminals.

Instrument voltage regulator on the back of a Series III speedometer.

minal on the back held in with a small screw that tends to come loose so that the terminal falls off.

◆ **Ignition switches:** Series II and IIA to 1967 have a combined ignition and light switch in the centre of the dash. These are durable but can suffer from corroded contacts on the back. Late Series IIA have a combined ignition/ starter switch in the dash centre and separate light switch, which seldom give trouble and are readily available. Series III petrol models incorporate a choke cable in the switch body. Diesels have an engine stop cable in the same place, with a latching mechanism to prevent the ignition from being switched off unless the engine stop knob is pulled out first. Both incorporate a steering lock attached to the steering column with shear bolts, which have to be drilled out to remove the lock assembly. The switch itself can be detached from the lock body and replaced (secured by two small screws through the edge) but the lock units are currently unavailable new. Later (90/110 or Defender) units will fit but do not have the fittings for the choke or engine stop cable, so if replacing them, a separate cable will have to be arranged.

◆ **Windscreen wipers do not self-park (Series IIA 1967 onwards, Series III):** there is a park switch built into the wiper motor, which frequently fails. It is accessible after removing the wiper motor cover and removed by pulling it outwards to clear the lug on the end and sliding to the left. Part number is 520160. A faulty park switch can also cause the fuse for the wipers to blow.

◆ **Switch failures:** the following items are intrinsically unreliable and will inevitably fail at some point: brake light switch (hydraulic, Series II/IIA 1958–67), brake light switch (mechanical, mounted on brake servo, Series IIA/ III where servo fitted), oil pressure light switch (all models), panel light switch (all models), hazard warning and fog-light switches (most later Series IIIs). The big metal MagnaTex indicator switches on Series IIAs are durable but many now suffer worn contacts due to sheer old age. The screenwash switch on the Series III has a spade ter-

ABOVE: A new park switch is cheap and easy to fit. It is retained by the spring clip visible here.

1967-onwards wiper motor showing park switch.

This kind of sub-standard home wiring is all too common on Series vehicles.

Wiring Loom

The main wiring loom will deteriorate with age: the insulating material cracks, copper wires oxidize and turn black, connecting terminals crumble to dust. Many vehicles have been badly butchered over the years with additional wiring spliced in, often with Scotchlock connectors or, worse, wires simply twisted together and wrapped in insulating tape. There may come a point where you spend so much time trying to pinpoint electrical faults, or worrying about whether your vehicle will catch fire when you switch the lights on, that it is better to bin the entire wiring loom and start again. This sounds daunting, but it is not.

New wiring looms are available to fit almost every variant of Series II, IIA and III Land Rovers. It does not always make sense to order a loom of the exact type that your vehicle had when it left the factory. For example, if the vehicle has been converted from diesel to petrol, it will be easier to buy a petrol loom (and whatever new switches are needed) than try to convert a diesel loom to suit the petrol engine that you now have. And if your 1961 vehicle now has a 1968 bulkhead and dash panel, a 1961-pattern loom will be of no use to you. The main variants are as follows:

◆ **Series II 1958–61:** screw terminals on most switches and ancillaries. Twin wiper motors attached to windscreen frame. Large separate oil and charge warning lights, ammeter and fuel gauge. Combined ignition/ lighting switch in centre of dash panel. Petrol models have starter button on firewall, diesels have tractor-type key switch under main dash panel.

◆ **Series IIA 1961–66:** spade terminals instead of screw.

◆ **Series IIA 1967–71:** black instrument panel with combined ignition/starter switch in centre on petrol and diesel models. Oil and charge warning lights built into instruments. Ammeter replaced by temperature gauge. Single wiper motor on left side of bulkhead, toggle switches for lights and wipers. 6-cylinder models have additional wiring for fuel pump and battery under passenger seat.

◆ **Series III 1971–85:** all-new design, instruments in front of driver. Additional circuits added during production run for fog-light, hazard flashers, brake check system, reversing lights.

The old loom is mostly very accessible for removal, requiring little more than taking out the instrument panel and (on a Series III) the parcel shelf tray. It is possible to order a wiring loom already fitted with additional wiring for hazard warning lights, alternator charging (Series II/IIA), reversing lights, front fog-lights and much more. The entire job can normally be done in a day. Probably the trickiest part is feeding the rear loom through the chassis rail: this can normally be done by taping the rear of the new loom to the front of the old one (having cut off the connectors) and drawing the new loom carefully through from front to back. Alternatively, you can run the loom along the outside of the chassis and secure it with cable ties: there is no harm in doing so.

As well as the new loom, you will need: securing 'P' clips with nuts, bolts, washers and self-tapping screws in a variety of sizes; a handful of black bullet joiners (two-way, four-way and possibly a couple of six-way at the back, depending on whether you have fog and reversing lights); possibly new side, tail and indicator light units, if your old ones are in poor condition; a box of assorted rubber grommets to protect the loom where it passes through sharp-edged holes; 6.3mm male bullet crimp connectors, crimp ring terminals, maybe a handful of spade connectors and some crimping pliers (new wiring looms never seem to

exactly match what was there originally); a good wiring diagram (obviously); and a ready supply of tea and biscuits. The headlight wiring harnesses do not come with the loom: order new ones unless yours are in really good shape.

Work methodically and ensure that the new wiring loom is properly secured and does not rub on sharp edges anywhere. When removing the old loom, do not disconnect the wires behind the dash panel, instead cut them off, leaving enough to be able to identify the wiring colours. Connecting up the dash panel is the most complicated part of the job, and it will save you a lot of time if you can see straight away which wire goes where, rather than trying to find the terminal numbers on the back of ancient Lucas switches.

Dashboard wiring on a Series III. This looks more intimidating than it is: an hour with a wiring diagram will see everything back together.

This chassis has rotted on all four faces and is beyond repair.

repairing corrosion

Old Land Rovers are not immortal. The body panels may be aluminium, but the chassis and bulkhead are made of good old-fashioned mild steel with minimal protection against corrosion. Unless your Land Rover has already acquired a galvanized chassis and bulkhead, sooner or later you will find holes. The rate at which old Land Rovers rust varies enormously, depending on when they were built, where they have spent their lives and what they were used for. Back in 1993, the author was offered a ten-year-old Series III with just 10,000 miles on the clock and whose chassis had almost completely disintegrated. It had spent its entire life in a factory that made corrosive chemicals.

As a general rule, the older the vehicle, the better the quality of steel used in its construction. There are many Series IIs and early IIAs out there that still have most of their original metalwork, with just the odd patch here and there. From the mid-1970s onwards, with the British steel industry beset by industrial strife, British Leyland started using steel from wherever they could find it. Some of it was Russian, contained a large proportion of recycled scrap and corroded very rapidly once the paint fell off it. Ex-military vehicles pose a different problem: when new they had a thick coat of rubberized underseal painted over the

chassis and bulkhead, which hardened and cracked with age. Water got in underneath and ate away unseen at the steel, until only the underseal was left. As a result, survival rates for ex-military Series vehicles are rather lower than you might expect.

But if you start poking around under your Land Rover and find holes, all is not lost. Repair sections are available for almost every part of the chassis, which is prone to rust, and for most of the bulkhead as well. Access is generally good, and the thickness of the steel used makes it relatively easy to weld in new metal, provided there is enough solid chassis left to weld to. So your first job will be to establish just how far the rot extends. Keep poking and scraping and hammering until you have established the awful truth. You do not want to be trying to weld to paper-thin, rusty metal or to have to come back and repair the same area a second time for the next MoT test.

Welding is a skill that can only be acquired with practice. Your first decision should be what kind of welder to acquire. In the old days, the choice would have been arc or gas. Arc welders were cheap but difficult to master, especially when trying to weld thin metal sections without blowing holes in them. Gas welding was gentler but far more expensive and

This appalling chassis 'repair' was hidden by the tool locker under the passenger seat.

required a good deal of skill. Then came MIG (metal inert gas) welding. In this process, welding wire is fed through a nozzle, along with an inert gas that prevents the weld from oxidizing. Compared to the two other processes, MIG welding is child's play. Once you have established the correct current, wire feed speed and gas flow for the thickness you need to weld, it is not much harder than drawing a line with a felt tip pen. Anyone can master it.

So, you will need a MIG welder, around 130–140A and fan-cooled unless you enjoy sitting around drinking tea while you wait for the thermal cut-out switch to reset itself. There are plenty to choose from at a reasonable price. You will also need a gas bottle. Forget the disposable bottles sold by car accessory shops – this is a horribly expensive way to

weld. You can either rent a large bottle from an industrial supplier, such as BOC, or buy a bottle on a non-rental basis, with a deposit refundable when you return it empty. For someone who only welds occasionally, the latter will usually be cheaper. You will also need a face shield, ideally the kind that automatically darkens when you start welding, and some protective gear – gauntlets at the very least and heavy flameproof overalls. Welding is dangerous. A blob of molten metal falling down your sleeve will burn you very badly in the time it takes to cool down. And a blob lodging in a dusty corner of your wood-framed garage will set the place on fire. Your new welder will come with detailed safety instructions: be sure to read them thoroughly at least twice before you even think about plugging in your new toy.

Metalworking tools: lots of clamps, and a hole punch.

Practice makes perfect. See if you can acquire some steel offcuts of various shapes and thicknesses, and spend a couple of hours trying to join them together. You are looking to create smooth, even welds that penetrate deep into the metal being welded, without burning holes in it. Until you can do this, it is not a good idea to start welding up your Land Rover. Cleanliness is vital. Rusty metal will weld badly, if at all, and your welds will be weak and full of tiny holes like a metallic Aero bar. Test your welds by bending them backwards and forwards: you will soon know whether they are strong enough to hold a ton and a half of Land Rover together.

Once you are confident that you can weld to an acceptable standard (and I mean acceptable to an MoT tester), you can start working out how to repair the rust in your Land Rover. The usual question is – patch or replace? For the main chassis rails, the only option will be to patch. For outriggers, crossmembers and front chassis legs, where repair sections are available, it will depend on the size of the hole, the soundness of the surrounding metal, the ease (or otherwise) with which the offending section can be cut out and, of course, how much time you are prepared to spend. Replacing a rear crossmember or front chassis leg will usually take far longer than patching, but faced with a bulkhead outrigger that is rotten on three sides, you may find it much quicker just to cut the whole thing off and start again.

Never weld patches over rust. It is pointless, unless you plan to dispose of the vehicle shortly afterwards. The rust will rapidly eat its way through your unprotected bare metal patch, and in a short time you will be back where you started. To carry out a satisfactory patch repair, the rot should be cut out until sound metal is reached. Cut a patch to a size that just overlaps the edges of the hole and weld continuously all the way round. As your skills improve, you will find yourself able to carry out near-invisible repairs, where the patch is set flush with the surrounding metal. However, you need to have a great deal of confidence in the ability of your welds to penetrate properly before you can start doing this. For now, stick to overlapping patches.

The thickness of the patch should be no less than that of the surrounding metal. I generally use 2.5mm or 3.0mm sheet steel

It is not just the chassis that rots. This is the rear axle casing on a Series II.

Rot in the bottom of the main chassis rail, caused by mud building up inside.

Rotten metal cut out, new steel welded in.

for this kind of repair. The idea is to restore the strength of the chassis, not just to hide problems from the MoT tester. Sheet steel in small quantities can be quite hard to obtain. Most steel stockholders will want to sell you a 2,400 × 1,200mm sheet, which is impossible to handle unless cut up into little bits. If you have a steel fabricator in your area, it is worth approaching them and asking whether you can buy some offcuts. Make sure you get mild steel, not stainless: the latter may sound like a good idea, but you will not be able to weld it with your hobby MIG.

POPULAR CHASSIS REPAIR SECTIONS

Front Chassis Legs (or 'Dumb Irons')   These replace the front end of the chassis rail, from the bumper to the front crossmember. They are designed to overlap the existing chassis rail, which is cut back to just forward of where the repair section will start. They have a tab on the inner face, which is supposed to ensure correct alignment, but from experience this tab is not always an accurate guide. The bumper and front spring will need to be removed. Accuracy is critical. Before cutting off the old leg, measure the height from the spring eye hole to the floor, the distance between the front and rear spring mounting holes, and the distance between the inside faces of the two chassis legs. These dimensions must be exactly reproduced or your Land Rover will lean to one side and the bumper will be askew. Position the new section, make a couple of small tack welds and re-measure. Do not start welding all round until you are absolutely certain that you have the dimensions spot-on.

Bulkhead Outriggers   Usually easy enough once you have removed the floor panel and freed the long bolt that secures the outrigger to the mounting foot. Most outriggers come attached to a rectangular flat plate: you will understand why when you cut off the old outrigger and find a big hole in the chassis rail behind it.

Fuel-Tank Outriggers/Rear Body Tub Outriggers   Easy enough to cut off and replace, but on vehicles with under-seat fuel tanks, the distance between the front and rear outriggers is critical. Get this wrong and your fuel tank will not fit. Never try to replace or repair a tank outrigger with the fuel tank in place, for obvious reasons.

Front of Rear Spring Hangers (Long Wheelbase)   Another common rot spot. The critical dimension here is the distance between the two spring mounting holes.

Rear of Rear Spring Hangers (Long Wheelbase)   As for front, with the additional complication that it is almost impossible to weld them along the top edge without either removing the rear body tub or cutting holes in the floor.

Rear of Rear Spring Hangers (Short Wheelbase)   These sit directly under the main chassis rail and you will usually find the entire area is rotten. A new quarter chassis is often a better bet.

Rear Crossmember   Can be bought plain or with U-shaped extensions that overlap the existing chassis rails. The latter is normally easier to fit. Again, the top face cannot readily be welded with the body tub in place unless you cut access holes in the floor. Alignment is important: the rear edge of the body tub will provide a guide (unless very badly bent) but you also need to make sure that the rear face of the crossmember is vertical. Use a straight edge down the back of the body tub and crossmember to check this. On later long-wheelbase vehicles, the fuel tank is bolted to the rear crossmember and will need to be removed. It is big and heavy, and the mounting bolts are hard to reach.

Quarter Chassis   Only available for short-wheelbase vehicles, this replaces the rear 18in or so of the chassis, including the crossmember and spring hangers. It is designed to sleeve over the existing chassis rails.

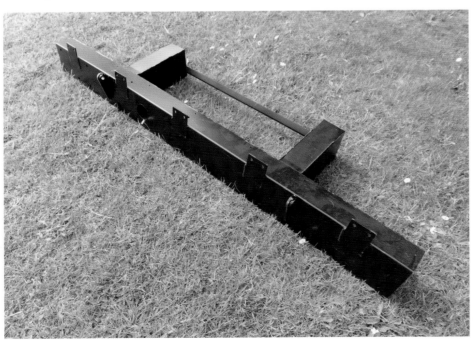

New military pattern rear crossmember with extensions.

This vehicle has had a replacement rear quarter chassis: note the vertical welded seam on the main chassis rail.

Half Chassis As for quarter chassis but also incorporates the body tub outriggers and extends forwards to just behind the centre crossmember. Big, heavy and very tricky to manoeuvre into place and support for welding. The rear body tub really has to come off to fit it. Get the positioning slightly wrong and your doors will never shut again. If your chassis is bad enough to need this much metal replacing, it might be time for a new one.

BULKHEAD REPAIRS

Just about any bulkhead is repairable, in theory, but some areas are much trickier than others. The most common rot spots are the footwells, door pillars and the mounting feet, which attach the pillars to the chassis. Repair sections are available for all of these and repairs are possible without removing the bulkhead from the vehicle – although to do the job properly, the front wings will need to come off. The wings are held on with a vertical row of fasteners at the front attaching them to the radiator panel, four bolts at the back holding the trailing edge to the door pillar, a single nut and bolt attaching the inner wing to the steering box mounting bracket, and some small nuts and bolts holding the bottom of the wing to the sill and the top rear edge to the front of the bulkhead. There are also steel mudshields under the wings that will need to be removed to gain access to the rear wing bolts, which are often badly rusted.

Replacement footwells normally come with the outer end already attached. The original footwells have strengthening ribs pressed into them and a reinforcing plate around the pedal boxes and steering box mounts. Cheap replacement footwells lack these features but it is now possible to buy good-quality panels that more closely follow the original design. The top section of the footwell is sandwiched between two pieces of steel with many, many spot welds holding it in place. To do the job properly, all these will need to be drilled out. However, if the top part of the footwell is sound, there is no need to replace the whole thing – the repair section can be cut down and just the rotten areas renewed. The outer panel wraps round the inside of the door pillar and will need to be welded to its trailing edge. This is normally done by drilling holes in the pillar, clamping the footwell in place and plug-welding the two sections together via the holes.

Patch repairs to an otherwise sound footwell.

Replacement footwell: a good-quality item with reinforcing ribs pressed in.

nut plates inside the door pillars, retained by a steel tab to stop them dropping down. These can be made quite easily, being simply a narrow steel strip with two nuts welded to it. Alternatively, the Series III-type clips can be used, but you will need either late-type Series IIA door hinges (with a hollow recess for the clips) or Series III hinges. The thread size on the Series III clips is $5/16$in UNF. The mounting foot should be plug welded to the base of the door pillar. Most of these vehicles have door seals riveted to the pillar, with a return lip to hold them in place. Replacement pillars have a simple, flat edge and are designed for the later clip-on door seals, which come in one piece and are far cheaper than the riveted type. To convert to the later-type seals, you will need to very carefully cut off the return lip all around the door aperture, using a 1mm cutting disc and a steady hand. As with the footwells, door pillars can be cut down, as required, but if the area around the top door hinge is sound, it is best left alone.

Before fully welding the new footwell, it is important to make sure that it is not twisted. The bottom edge should be parallel to the front edge of the seat box, otherwise the floor panel will not fit properly. It is quite common to see vehicles where the new footwell has simply been popped over the top of the rusty old one and welded around the edge. Some people do not even bother with welding and just use pop rivets. This is not strong enough: the footwell is part of the supporting structure for the brake pedal and steering box and is not an area that should be bodged. For small, localized areas of rot, it is perfectly acceptable to cut out the affected area and weld in a patch. It is not a good idea just to weld patches over rot, as they will rust through within a short space of time.

Door pillars come in two parts: the pillar itself, and the mounting foot. Replacement can be tricky. It is vital that the two pillars are parallel to each other and the correct distance apart (64in across the outer face of the pillars). Series III Land Rovers use captive nuts on clips to retain the door hinges and allow for adjustment. Earlier vehicles use captive

Moving further up, rot in the top outer corners of the bulkhead is quite common. 'Repair' sections are available, but these are designed to be welded over the top of the rot to hide it, rather than to actually replace the rotten area. It is much better to cut out all the rot and weld in new metal. Rot along the top edge of the bulkhead under the windscreen or around the fresh air vents is much harder to tackle, as the metal here is very thin and hard to weld without distorting it. The top inner corners are also prone to rust. On a Series II or IIA bulkhead, this area supports the windscreen-retaining clamps and can be tricky to repair. A bulkhead that is severely rotted anywhere above the top of the footwells will be very difficult to repair properly, as the rot is likely to have got into the internal strengthening sections, which are completely inaccessible; replacement may be the only option.

improving your Land Rover: reliability and on-road performance

The basic design of these vehicles is now almost sixty years old, and in some ways it shows. Even a very late Series III can be, quite literally, a pain to live with. But a massive industry has grown up around the supply of parts to improve these vehicles, making them more comfortable, more reliable and more capable, both on- and off-road. There are limits to what can be done: although it is technically possible to build up a Series II that drives as well as a Defender, to do so will end up costing far more than buying a good Defender in the first place. To some extent you have to accept these vehicles for what they are – a simple, no-nonsense workhorse with bags of period charm. But there is a good deal that can be done to make your Land Rover easier to live with, without destroying its distinctive character. Improvements fall broadly into four categories: reliability, on-road performance, comfort and off-road performance. This chapter and the next will look at each of these in turn.

RELIABILITY

These vehicles are simple, well engineered and will provide dependable service, provided that they are properly maintained. This is a point that is often overlooked. They need regular maintenance and do not always get it. So, on a newly acquired vehicle, a full service, with replacement of components that are obviously near the end of their life, should be your starting point. Having said this, automotive technology has come a long way since the last Series III rolled out of the factory thirty years ago, and there are a few things you can do to minimize the chance of your vehicle letting you down:

Ignition   The points ignition system on petrol engines needs regular attention and adjustment and is responsible for around 90 per cent of all starting and running problems with these vehicles. For greater reliability you should consider fitting electronic ignition. There are two basic types:

◆ **Optical type** – sold for many years by Lumenition and still available. The original distributor is retained, but with the points replaced with a photo-transistor and a segmented 'chopper' wheel positioned beneath the rotor arm. This sends a signal to a separate control box, which in turn generates the spark. It is a proven, reliable system and still available new.
◆ **Magnetic type** – the points are replaced with a magnetic pickup, which takes its signal from a sleeve over the distributor shaft. The pickup is connected directly to the ignition coil with no separate control box. This type can either be purchased as a kit to fit an existing distributor, or as a complete brand-new distributor.

Self-contained electronic ignition system, with the electronics hidden inside the distributor body.

Zenith 36IV carburettor, factory fit for 4-cylinder engines 1967–85.

It is worth remembering that while a failed points ignition system can often be poked back into life with a bit of cleaning and adjustment, there is nothing you can do at the roadside to resurrect a faulty electronic unit. It is worth hanging on to the bits that you removed to fit the electronic system and keeping them in a bag inside the vehicle just in case.

Carburettors The original equipment Solex (to 1966) and Zenith (1967 onwards) carburettors on 4-cylinder engines are simple beasts and reliable if in good order, but many are now badly worn. Many vehicles have been retrofitted with the Weber 34ICH carburettor, which is marketed as an economy-enhancing device. A new Weber will certainly give better fuel economy than a badly worn original, but it is a little small for the job and tends to suffer from icing in cold weather. Cheap replacement Zenith carburettors are also available: the quality of these is not always what it should be. In general, you will be better off having your original carburettor rebuilt by a specialist. Early Land Rover Ninety and One Ten models had the same 2286cc petrol engine as the late Series III, but with a twin-choke Weber carburettor on a redesigned manifold; this carburettor works very well when in good order, but fitting is not straightforward. You will need to convert to cable-operated throttle, fabricate a new exhaust downpipe and fit an electric fuel pump in place of the mechanical one.

Diesels The heater plugs on these engines are wired in series, so that if one fails, the entire system stops working and the engine will be almost impossible to start from cold. Kits are available to convert to modern parallel-wired heater plugs and fitting is very easy.

Additional Gauges

The instrumentation in Series' vehicles is very basic. Vehicles built before 1967 do not even have a coolant temperature gauge fitted as standard. Auxiliary gauges are widely available and easy to fit. On a Series II or IIA they can be mounted to an aluminium panel attached on either side of the main dash panel: the Series III has room for up to three gauges in the centre of the lower dashboard. The most popular additional gauges are:

◆ **Coolant temperature:** these can be either mechanical, using a capillary tube running from a sender bulb direct to the gauge, or electrical, with a temperature sender unit screwed into the cylinder head and attached to the gauge by a single wire. The latter type is usually less fiddly to instal. Almost all the 4-cylinder engines have a blanking plug near the thermostat housing (petrol) or on top of the cylinder head towards the back (diesel), which can be unscrewed to allow fitment of the sender unit. You will need the appropriate threaded adapter; aftermarket gauges usually come with a selection. The temperature gauge from a later Land Rover Ninety or One Ten can also be used, together with the sender unit from a 2.5 diesel (part number PRC2505), which will fit the 2.25 cylinder head.

◆ **Oil pressure:** again available in either mechanical or electrical versions. Installation requires a 'T' adapter, which screws into the oil filter housing in place of the existing pressure switch, allowing both the switch and the sender to share the same oil supply. The oil pressure switch on the 2.25 and 2.6 engines is threaded ⅜in BSF, which is not a very common size for pressure switches. Land Rover made a 'banjo' adapter kit at one time to suit, but these are now quite rare. The 109 V8 had an oil pressure gauge fitted as standard.

◆ **Voltmeter:** gives a useful early warning of problems with the charging system, allowing you to do something before the battery goes flat. When an alternator fails, it is quite common for the charge warning light to stop working. A voltmeter is simply connected to a switched feed on one side and a suitable earth on the other.

◆ **Oil temperature:** often found on ex-military vehicles. To fit one to a civilian vehicle, you will need to remove the sump and weld or braze in a threaded boss to take the sender unit, unless you can find a sump from an ex-military engine that already has this fitting. Only really useful if your Land Rover spends a lot of time running flat out on the motorway or towing heavy loads in hot weather.

◆ **Vacuum gauge (petrol engines):** displays the inlet manifold vacuum when the engine is running. Once popular as an aid to economical driving: the wider you open the throttle, the less the vacuum. Gauges are often marked with green, yellow and red segments, the idea being to keep the needle in the green sector. Usually mechanical, connects to the pipe between the inlet manifold and brake servo (where fitted) using a T-adapter.

ON-ROAD PERFORMANCE

The engines fitted to these vehicles are not especially efficient and you will find that you have to spend quite a lot of money for a relatively small power gain. This especially applies to the diesel, for which there are no commercially available tuning parts. The 4-cylinder petrol engine is a slightly better proposition for tuning; as supplied, it is in a very low state of tune with a low compression ratio and rather restrictive manifolds. It is possible to get another 30–35bhp out of one of these engines, but at a cost: gas-flowed high-compression cylinder head, new manifolds and a re-profiled camshaft will soon add up to a large bill. Before you start spending money, it is worth remembering that many of these engines, through wear or neglect, develop far less power than Land Rover intended. A good, healthy 2.25 petrol-engined Land Rover feels surprisingly frisky, and even a well-sorted diesel will keep up with the traffic quite happily – most of the time.

SU carburettor and tubular exhaust manifold on a 2.25 petrol engine. Tuning parts are not cheap.

Intake restrictors on the V8 are accessible after removing the carburettors.

The 109 V8 was heavily detuned by fitting cast aluminium restrictor blocks inside the manifold intakes. These are held in with snap rings and can be pulled out after removing the carburettors, giving you an extra 40bhp (and, strangely, better fuel economy) for the cost of a few gaskets.

If you are really determined to improve your Land Rover's on-road performance, the most cost-effective route (especially if your engine is worn and tired) will be to replace it with a larger and more powerful one. Some of the more popular conversions are:

◆ **2.5 petrol (Land Rover Ninety/One Ten)** – will fit in place of any 2286cc petrol or diesel engine, but the carburettor and manifolds are completely different. A little rougher than the 2.25 but cheap, pulls strongly from low revs and is unleaded-compatible.

◆ **2.5 diesel (Land Rover Ninety/One Ten)** – available in either turbo or non-turbo versions. Offside engine mounting bracket will need to be cut and welded to clear the injection pump, and the battery relocated. The turbo-diesel has a poor reputation for durability but works well in these vehicles when in good condition.

◆ **200TDi turbo-diesel (Land Rover Defender/Discovery)** – Defender version has a low-mounted injection pump and needs the same chassis modifications as the older 2.5 diesel. Discovery variant will fit the standard Series chassis mounts but needs modifications to the flywheel housing, and the turbocharger fouls the chassis rail on long-wheelbase models. Excellent performance, economy and durability, but very noisy. Sometimes fitted without turbo ('200Di'), which simplifies installation and gives about the same performance as a healthy 2.25 petrol, with far better fuel economy.

◆ **300TDi turbo-diesel (Land Rover Defender/Discovery)** – needs new chassis mounts and modified 2.5 diesel flywheel housing. Clearance is very tight at the front for coolant hoses. Turbocharger mounted higher up than a 200TDi, so will fit long-wheelbase vehicles.

◆ **Rover V8** – once very popular and still has a following. Needs adapter plate to mate to the gearbox, modifications to the footwells and a remote oil filter (the standard one fouls the front axle).

◆ **Ford Transit 2.5Di** – torquey, durable, very economical but noisy engine, requires footwell cutting and welding, among other things.

◆ **Perkins Prima** – 2.0 turbo-diesel from an Austin Montego. Needs quite a lot of work to fit and some parts now getting hard to find.

◆ **Perkins 4.203** – heavy, plodding agricultural engine, a popular conversion at one time, although now out of fashion. Very slow-revving, noisy, needs 3.54 axles and an overdrive to achieve a decent cruising speed.

A few more horses under the bonnet: 200TDi engine removed from a rusty Discovery and shoehorned into a 1967 Series IIA.

This is a 200Di (Tdi sans turbocharger): not as powerful as a Tdi, but simpler to fit.

6-cylinder vehicles are far more difficult to convert than 'fours': the engine sits further back in the chassis and the bellhousing bolt pattern is different, as are the engine mounting brackets. Some engine conversion kits (including Rover V8 and Perkins 4.203) were manufactured specifically for 6-cylinder installations: these are no longer available new but still occasionally turn up second-hand. The early 3-litre version of the straight-six engine from a Rover P5 saloon can be made to fit easily enough and gives 115bhp, but the later 134bhp Weslake-head version (with the inlet manifold separate from rather than cast into the head) requires some ingenuity to achieve adequate clearance for the carburettor. These cars are still popular with banger racers, so 3-litre engines are not impossible to find.

Braking Systems

If you are going to put a significantly more powerful engine into your Land Rover, you need to think about how you will stop. Series vehicles have acquired a reputation for poor brakes. This is not really the vehicles' fault – much of the perceived poor performance is caused by lack of maintenance and the use of cheap substandard replacement parts. However, the braking system design underwent several changes over the years, so it is worth looking at the various differences to see what can be done to upgrade the older vehicles.

Most Series vehicles had one of two types of braking system: 109in vehicles, and 88in from mid-1980 onwards, had 11in front brakes of the twin leading shoe (TLS) type. This is a pretty good system and when in good condition should be more than enough for most people's needs. Pre-1980 88in vehicles had 10in single leading shoe (SLS) brakes, which are a little more marginal. They will cope fine with a lightly laden vehicle driven at modern speeds, but emergency braking, downhill and fully laden, may find them wanting. Having said that, the 10in SLS brakes seem to require less maintenance than the 11in TLS system and

---

LPG ('AUTOGAS') CONVERSIONS

Liquid petroleum gas (LPG), sometimes known as 'Autogas', has become increasingly popular in recent years. The 'two and a quarter' takes quite readily to running on LPG provided it has been fitted with hardened valve seats, and the V8 will run on LPG without modification. An LPG system normally consists of a large cylindrical tank, a vaporizer unit (mounted under the bonnet and plumbed into the cooling system), a diffuser mounted in the air intake as close as possible to the carburettor and a control unit inside the vehicle to switch between petrol and LPG.

You will lose a little power and economy (around 10 per cent), and you will need at least a 22gal (100ltr) tank to provide usable range, which will take up a lot of interior space. Twin or even triple underslung tanks of smaller size can often be accommodated somewhere underneath the vehicle but greatly increase the conversion cost and can be vulnerable to damage off-road. But with LPG currently around half the cost of unleaded, if you are using your Land Rover as daily transport, the conversion will pay for itself in a fairly short time. Resist the temptation to replace the main petrol tank with a small 'emergency' tank to make more space for the LPG system: not all filling stations sell LPG, and two gallons of petrol may not be enough to get you to the next one that does.

On most Series II and IIA vehicles, the wing top has to be cut back to fit a servo unit.

are a lot simpler to work on. It is possible to convert earlier 88in vehicles to the TLS system, but the brake master cylinder will need to be changed to the 109in type.

Servo assistance was available as an option on the 109in Series III, and was fitted as standard to Station Wagons and to later 88in vehicles. With a servo fitted, the brakes require far less pressure to operate, and in modern traffic conditions it is well worth having. It is possible to retrofit a Series III brake servo to almost any Series vehicle, but it really needs to be fitted in conjunction with the TLS front brakes or a dual-circuit braking system. Land Rover never made servo brakes available with the single-circuit SLS

system, so there is no suitable master cylinder available. To fit a Series III servo to a Series II or IIA, the offside front wing needs to be cut back, and a new underwing mudshield fitted. As an alternative, on vehicles with single-circuit brakes it is possible to fit an aftermarket in-line servo, which avoids the need to cut the wing and allows the vehicle to be returned easily to original unmodified condition. This option will work with the SLS brakes. The servo fitted to earlier MGB sports cars is ideal and readily available new. It must be mounted with the plastic valve on the body facing downwards, or the brakes will be impossible to bleed.

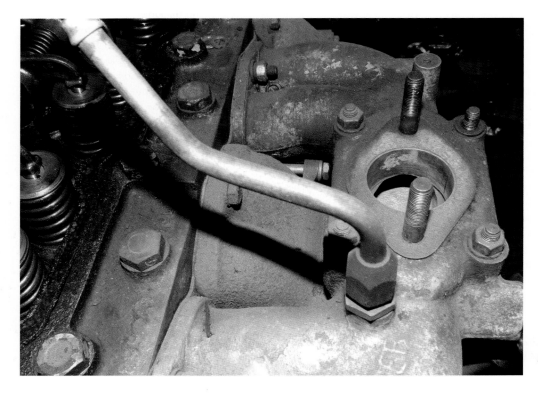

Brake servo vacuum pipe on a 2.25 petrol manifold.

Diesels used this butterfly valve attached to the air intake to create vacuum for the brake servo: a not entirely successful design.

On petrol engines, the servo is powered by vacuum from the inlet manifold. Most engines have a blanking plug on top of the manifold that can be removed and a suitable connecting pipe and adapter fitted in their place. Early 2.25 engines lack this blanking plug, so the manifold will have to be removed and either drilled and tapped for the adapter, or replaced with one from a later engine. For the diesel engine, Land Rover designed a complex system with a butterfly valve in the inlet manifold, a vacuum tank mounted to the nearside inner wing and various pipes and one-way valves. The theory was that when descending a hill with the throttle closed, the butterfly valve would create a vacuum in the manifold, which was then stored in the tank, in turn providing a reserve supply for the servo. In practice, the system proved inefficient and fiddly to set up. Early Land Rover One Tens had the same 2.25 diesel engine but with a belt-driven vacuum pump but parts for this installation are now very hard to find. Some modern cars (including certain variants of the Volvo S60 saloon) have an electrically powered vacuum pump operated by a pressure-sensing switch. Such a system should provide the perfect solution to the problem of powering a brake servo on a 2.25 diesel Land Rover, and a visit to a scrapyard may prove fruitful.

Up to 1980, Land Rovers generally had single-circuit brake hydraulics. In this system, if a component fails (such as a burst pipe), all the fluid will be lost, resulting in total brake failure. Post-1980 vehicles had dual-circuit brakes, where the hydraulics are split into two separate circuits (front and rear), each with its own fluid supply. This is a much safer system, as a loss of fluid in one circuit will not lead to total loss of brakes. The dual-circuit system can be retrofitted to earlier vehicles, but the appropriate master cylinder can only be fitted to servo-equipped vehicles. Dual-circuit, servo and 11in TLS front brakes will be about as good as you are going to get with Land Rover components. If you still need more performance (for example,

if you have a V8-powered vehicle or tow heavy trailers in hilly areas), you might need to think about the disc brake conversions that are available from various suppliers

Higher Gearing

All the Series' vehicles are under-geared for road use, with first gear being redundant unless you are stationary with a heavy trailer behind you on a steep hill. There are several ways in which you can raise the gearing for a more relaxed cruise (and better fuel economy). The cheapest, but least satisfactory, is to replace the 4.7 ratio differentials with 3.54 items. This increases the gearing by around 33 per cent, but the speedo reading will then be out by the same amount and the effectiveness of the handbrake is very much decreased. The low ratio gearing is also raised 33 per cent, reducing off-road capability. And depending on how much power your engine is producing, you may run into problems due to the large ratio gap between third and fourth gear. Increasing the overall gearing also increases the size of this gap. You end up screaming the engine in third gear; drop it into fourth and the power drops away. On long hills, you are forever swapping between third and fourth to maintain reasonable progress. High ratio differentials work well with V8s, turbo-diesels (especially the TDi) or big, old diesels like the Perkins 4.203. They are also fine in a short wheelbase with a good healthy 2.25 petrol engine. But for a tired petrol, or 2.25 diesel, or a long wheelbase (especially a Station Wagon), you may be disappointed.

Also very popular is an overdrive unit – basically a two-speed gearbox that bolts onto the back of the standard four-speed box. When engaged, this gives around 30 per cent increase in gearing. The 'Fairey' (later Superwinch) overdrive is by far the most popular, and is widely available second-hand; but it does have a couple of problems. The oil capacity is small and many of these units have been damaged by overheating through running low on oil. It is not an especially robust unit and can be broken through misuse (most commonly, using first and second gear with

The black knob controls a Fairey overdrive: push forwards to engage.

The Fairey overdrive bolts to the back of the transfer box. Minor oil leaks are endemic to these units.

This rear cover on the transfer box, and the gear behind it, are removed to fit an overdrive unit.

the overdrive engaged). Parts availability is very poor. These overdrives can get very noisy when the bearings wear. There are far more bad Faireys out there than good ones, making them a dubious second-hand purchase.

You might come across a 'Toro' overdrive – a close copy of the Fairey but with some small internal differences. They suffer the same problems as the Fairey unit and parts supply is non-existent. If you are looking at an overdrive that looks like a Fairey but has no maker's name on it, it may be a Toro – so beware. More recently, Rocky Mountain (a Canadian company) introduced the Roverdrive, an all-new design that uses the transfer box oil for lubrication. And Heystee (based in the Netherlands) now offers a substantially improved and strengthened version of the old Fairey design.

Finally, conversion kits are available from Ashcroft Transmissions to raise the high-range gearing in the transfer box. This gives a similar step up to the Fairey overdrive, but in all gears, all the time – so that first gear will finally get some use. Cost is quite reasonable (although there is a lot of labour required to fit one) and the conversion does not add any more moving parts to the drivetrain, which is good from a reliability point of view. Speedometer accuracy and handbrake efficiency are not affected. But although low ratio gearing is the same as before, high ratio is raised in much the same way as fitting 3.54 differentials, so the same warnings apply.

The 109 V8 already has 3.54 differentials but a very low-geared transfer box. An overdrive was available from Fairey for a while but these are rare and hard to find nowadays, and parts availability is even poorer than for the other Fairey overdrives. The old four-speed Range Rover (1971–82) used the same LT95 gearbox but with different transfer gearing. The high-range gears in the transfer box can be swapped for Range Rover items. This requires removal of the rear output housing and centre differential, but can be done without removing the entire transmission unit from the vehicle and makes a huge difference to cruising capability and fuel economy.

Free-Wheeling Hubs

These turn up quite often on old Land Rovers. They are designed to replace the front drive flanges, and contain a sliding splined member, usually operated by turning a knob or nut on the end of the hub, designed so that the hub can be disconnected from the halfshaft when driving on-road in two-wheel drive. This reduces drag, giving a slight improvement in fuel consumption and also saves some wear on the front halfshafts, differential and prop-shaft. The main disadvantage is that they have to be manually engaged when four-wheel drive is to be used. Self-engaging free-wheeling hubs were available for a short time in the 1970s but were expensive and not commercially successful. These hubs were made by a number of different companies including Fairey, Mayflower and AVM, and were available in either ten or twenty-four spline versions to suit the two different types of halfshaft fitted to Series vehicles. If a vehicle is fitted with these hubs, they should be engaged and the vehicle driven in two-wheel drive for several miles each month, as the upper steering swivel pin depends on splash lubrication from the rotating halfshaft.

Electric Cooling Fan

This is another popular modification, often marketed as an aid to fuel economy, and replaces the fixed belt-driven fan on the engine with an electric unit either directly in front of or behind the radiator, controlled by a thermostatic switch, which activates the fan when the coolant temperature exceeds a certain point. An electric fan has the advantage that it can be switched off for deep wading (see Chapter 14) and also allows the engine to warm up a little more quickly in cold weather. A good-quality electric fan will also be far more effective than a mechanical fan in keeping temperatures down when stuck in a traffic jam on a hot day.

Towing a Trailer

Almost all Series Land Rovers have a strong, deep, sturdy, box-section rear crossmember with substantial attachment points for a tow hitch. The exception is vehicles built to military specification, which have a much shallower crossmember. The bottom edge of the crossmember is much higher than the drawbar on most trailers, so you will need to fit a drop plate, either the standard Land Rover fixed plate or an adjustable-height drop plate. In either case, the drop plate should always be fitted in conjunction with the piece of angled steel that bolts to the bottom of the crossmember and the rear face of the drop plate. It should be obvious that the crossmember itself must be in good condition and free from rot if you are to tow safely. The tow ball should be adequately rated for the weight you plan to tow, and firmly attached with 16mm high-tensile steel bolts and locking nuts.

How much can you tow? This is a slightly controversial question in Land Rover enthusiast circles. The guidance given by the factory over the years was vague and often conflicting. On Series II and IIA vehicles, there is no indication on the vehicle as to the maximum permissible towing weight. Series IIIs up to 1979 bear the words 'recommended maximum towing capacity 2 tons' on the chassis plate. Post-1979 vehicles with the later British Leyland chassis plate indicate a maximum towing capacity for all Series III variants of 4,000kg (3.6 tons), although by law any trailer with a maximum gross weight above 3,500kg (3.15 tons) must be fitted with a braking system coupled to the vehicle brakes.

In practice, the '2 tons' figure is probably about as much as you are going to want to tow behind a vehicle with limited power and drum brakes all round. A 109 V8 has larger front brakes than lesser models, will pull the side off a house, if in good order, and should cope with 3 tons or more, but

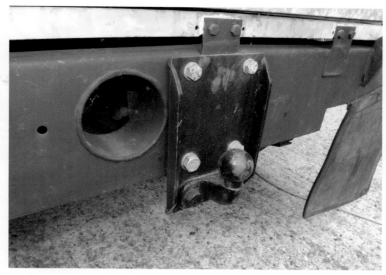

Standard short drop plate and tow hitch: only just deep enough for an 88in vehicle on standard tyres.

a short-wheelbase vehicle, being fairly light, can easily be pushed around by a heavy trailer on the back, especially if the weight is poorly distributed. It is also important to remember that on vehicles with 11in twin leading shoe front brakes, the braking power for a given pedal effort diminishes greatly when going backwards. When reversing, the overrun brakes on the trailer will also be inoperative. More than one luckless Series owner has tried reversing a heavy trailer down a steep slope and been unable to press the brake pedal hard enough to avoid ending up in a crumpled heap at the bottom.

Any Series vehicle can be used for towing, but for heavy loads the 109 V8 is best.

improving your Land Rover: comfort and off-road performance

COMFORT

A standard Series II, IIA or III Land Rover could never be described as comfortable. Crashing ride, deafening noise, unsupportive seats and heavy controls are all part of the classic Land Rover experience. This is all very well if your Land Rover is just a weekend toy, but quickly becomes tedious on a long journey. So what can you do to make your vehicle just a little easier to live with?

Parabolic Springs

One of the worst features of most 'Series' vehicles, is the bone-jarring ride. This is not entirely the fault of Land Rover. These vehicles use multi-leaf springs with oil-filled dampers, which were state-of-the-art technology back in 1948 and still have the advantages of strength and utter simplicity. When in good condition they work well enough,

although they tend to be rather bad at absorbing very large bumps. But they deteriorate badly with age: rust forms between the spring leaves and stops them sliding smoothly against each other, which locks the springs solid. This kind of deterioration does not usually result in an MoT failure, so there are many thousands of Land Rovers running around on really terrible springs.

Recent advances in leaf-spring technology provide an answer in the shape of parabolic springs, which are widely used on new vans and trucks. These have a smaller number of thicker leaves, which are specially shaped and touch only in the middle and at the ends. They do not suffer from the rusting problems of standard springs and have a longer travel, providing a better ride on bumpy ground and more traction off-road. They are available from several suppliers in a variety of different load capacities to suit different uses. They should be fitted in conjunction with uprated dampers to make the most of their superior ride capability.

Parabolic three-leaf rear springs: note how the leaves do not touch except at the ends and centre.

A simple door lining is effective in reducing noise levels.

Noise Reduction

There are two different ways in which this can be tackled. The traditional – and cheapest – way is to use sound-deadening felt, which is glued to the bulkhead, seat box, underside of the bonnet and sometimes the inside of the rear body, combined with heavy rubber floor mats. Felt-based soundproofing tends to peel away at the corners, looks quite scruffy in a short time and if you need to

remove it for any reason, it falls to bits and leaves a horrible hairy mess stuck to the inside of your Land Rover. A better alternative is the acoustic matting system developed by Wright Off Road and based on the technology used in large excavators and earth-moving machinery. This consists of a one-piece cast polyurethane mat that covers the floors, footwells and transmission tunnel, and another piece that covers the seat box. It makes a huge difference to noise levels, can be hosed down to get rid of the mud and looks

Full length headlining and air vents in a Station Wagon. The complete roof panel from a Station Wagon will bolt on in place of the standard hard-top roof.

The classic Smiths 'fug-stirrer' heater found on most Series II and IIA vehicles.

great. It is a bit fiddly to fit and awkward to remove once in place, but takes out a lot of the noise from the engine and transmission.

Another source of noise is the unlined metal doors. You can make a great deal of difference quite cheaply by fitting internal door liners – either vinyl-covered trims or, for the impecunious, a simple sheet of hardboard – and stuffing loft insulation material between the liner and the door skin. The metal roof on hard-top and truck-cab vehicles resonates and reflects noise. Factory-fitted headlinings are very rare, apart from on Station Wagons where they were standard. The best solution is to glue sound-absorbing material to the inside of the roof, ideally using 13mm closed-cell acoustic foam, which is quite readily available by the metre. It will take you some time if you want to make a really neat job of it – sticky sheets of foam are not easy to handle – but the reduction in noise will be well worth the effort. A heavy rubber mat over the rear load area is another simple modification that will make a big difference.

Finally, and once all your soundproofing is in place, listen for rattles inside the vehicle, identify the cause and fix them. Common rattle spots are loose sliding windows (will usually need the channels replacing), main gear lever (grease the pivot ball), transfer lever (tighten the securing nut and bolt that attaches the lever to the gearbox), underseat cover plates (line the edges with foam draught-excluder) and insecure floor panels (replace any missing screws).

Heating

The standard Series heaters are not great, and their demisting performance is especially feeble. There is not a huge amount that can be done about this, beyond flushing out the matrix with water to remove any sediment and, on Series III vehicles, ensuring that the flexible trunking between the blower fan and heater unit is intact and not full of holes. However, it is now possible to replace the standard front windscreens with electrically heated items, which use very fine filaments embedded in the glass, like a lot of modern cars. These make a big difference on cold, winter mornings, and by blanking off the standard demisting ducts, you will find that the performance of the heater is improved. On these vehicles, the screens are held in place with black mastic, aluminium strips and lots of small screws: replacement is well within the capabilities of the home mechanic, although it is much easier to do so with the windscreen frame removed from the vehicle.

Better Seats

It is always nice to have a bit of comfort on a long journey, but the original Series seats do not provide it. It is possible to replace them with high-back seats that fit the original Series seat frames and runners. Alternatively, you can fit a set of seats from a later Defender, which will bolt straight to the seat box after removing the old runners. The Defender seat design actually appeared first on late model Series III 'County' vehicles in about 1981. Land Rover seats have an unusually shallow base, as they are mounted on the seat box as opposed to most cars where the seats are bolted to the floorpan. As a result, there are very few car seats that will fit in a Land Rover and still allow you to get your knees under the steering wheel. Car seats also have fixed bases, making it impossible to access the tool locker under the passenger seat.

The centre front seat in a Land Rover is fairly useless for anything more than very short journeys and is often removed and replaced with a lockable cubby box. This provides a great place to store all the junk and rubbish that you would throw away if you did not have a cubby box to put it in.

Retracting Seat Belts

Inertia reel seatbelts were only supplied as standard on late Series IIIs but can be retrofitted to almost all Series Land Rovers. They are especially useful on Series II and IIA models, where the switchgear is scattered across the centre dash and is almost impossible to reach while wearing a correctly adjusted static seatbelt. It is important to use the correct brackets and spreader plates; some of the DIY installations out there would tear the mounts straight out of the body in a serious accident.

The exact method of fitting will vary according to the vehicle. On soft-top vehicles there is no strong point for the upper belt support, so you will have to mount the inertia reel onto the bulkhead behind the seat and put up with the belt rubbing on your shoulder. Truck-cab vehicles are also difficult: factory mounts are rare and, on a short-wheelbase vehicle, there is not enough space to mount the reel low down behind the seats. For hard-top vehicles there is an angled bracket that bolts between the front and top of each side panel and provides a strong anchor point for the upper mount.

Seat belt brackets bolt into the front upper corners of the hard top.

Vehicles manufactured prior to 1967 were not required to be fitted with seat belts, so there are quite a few older Land Rovers that have never had belts of any kind. It is still legal to drive a pre-1967 vehicle without seat belts, although if belts are fitted, they must be worn.

Doors

The standard doors fitted to all of these vehicles are of two-piece construction, with aluminium skins over steel frames and detachable door tops with sliding windows.

The second-row doors on Station Wagons are made in one piece. The doors are vulnerable to rust, especially along the bottom of the lower frames and around the base of the tops, where they bolt to the bottoms; this weakens the structure and allows the door top to flap around. The channels for the sliding windows are made of mild steel covered in felt, which gradually rust and disintegrate, either jamming the windows or allowing them to fall out altogether. The sliding rear side-windows in Station Wagons suffer from the same problem.

All-aluminium door tops are far stronger than the originals and have plastic channels that will not rot. They also allow both panes of glass to be moved; on the standard door top, only the rear pane is movable. Aluminium door tops can be purchased new from Rocky Mountain, or you can try to track down a pair of door tops from a military Defender, which are of similar construction to the Rocky Mountain ones. Alternatively, the doors can be replaced with later one-piece Defender doors with wind-up windows. These will fit the existing door apertures and hinges, but you will need to replace the striker plates at the front of the rear body tub to suit the Defender door catches and also arrange a suitable fixing for the door check straps, so that your new doors do not blow open in the wind and leave a big dent in the door pillar. The doors are a lot thicker than Series ones to make room for the winding mechanism, which restricts elbow room. Defender doors are quite expensive new and suffer from the same rot problems as Series doors, so tend to be hard to find second-hand at a sensible price.

Military door tops will bolt straight on to replace the rot-prone originals.

One-piece doors from a Ninety, One Ten or Defender will fit earlier vehicles.

Mirrors

Most of these vehicles left the factory with tiny mirrors mounted on stalks on the front wings. Some Series IIIs had door-mounted mirrors attached to a bracket sandwiched between the door and the hinge. Any of these vehicles can be converted to take the much larger, and easily adjustable, Defender mirrors, which attach via screws through two holes in the top hinge. If your hinge does not have these holes, it can either be drilled or swapped for a Defender hinge. Note that when fitting Defender/Series III door

Defender door mirror and hinge will fit a Series II or IIA.

hinges to a Series II or IIA, both top and bottom hinges must be changed, as the pivot point differs between the two types. For Series II and IIA it is possible to obtain a special top hinge with a cast lug to take a mirror stalk. These are quite rare and expensive but allow you to keep the protruding hinges, which many people see as part of the vehicle's character.

Power Steering

One of the most commonly asked questions from owners of older Land Rovers, is 'How can I fit power steering?' The steering system on these vehicles is unassisted but low-geared with a large-diameter steering wheel for more leverage, and should not be unduly heavy if all the components are in good condition. Problems sometimes arise when people fit oversized tyres or a small-diameter 'sports' steering wheel, either of which will make your Land Rover very hard work in car parks. The low gearing is also not ideal for off-road trialling, needing a great deal of steering wheel twirling to negotiate obstacles.

These vehicles have the steering box and column incorporated into a single unit, which makes it very difficult to fit a higher-geared steering system. There are a few conversions around, usually using a Defender steering column and a Range Rover steering box bolted to the outside of the chassis. You should be very wary of these. A power steering box puts an enormous amount of stress on its mounting points and will try to twist the chassis leg under load. It is very hard to be sure, on a home-brewed conversion, that the steering box mountings will not fatigue and fracture in use. Such conversions are also of dubious legality, as they involve a major structural change to the chassis.

The only system currently available, which can be guaranteed to be safe and legal, is that manufactured by Heystee to fit 4-cylinder vehicles. This uses a hydraulic ram acting on the drag link and a pump on a bracket specially made to fit the 2.25 engine. If the system fails, the steering continues to operate as normal (apart from becoming heavier) and the power assistance makes it possible to fit a smaller steering wheel, if you so wish.

Clutch Assistance

Although hydraulic, the clutch pedal on these vehicles is much heavier than on more modern vehicles. The 9in coil spring clutch fitted to most Series II and IIA vehicles with the 2.25 petrol engine is much heavier in operation than the 9½in diaphragm unit found on diesels and Series IIIs. An excessively heavy clutch pedal can also be caused by the flexible hose in the hydraulic system starting to break up internally. It is possible to replace the clutch pedal box with one from a Defender 300TDi or TD5: this has the same dimensions as the Series' pedal box, uses the same master cylinder and incorporates an over-centre spring to reduce pedal effort.

Wheels and Tyres

Any off-road vehicle is only as good as its tyres. The choice of tyres will always be a compromise between on- and off-road ability. Chunky off-road tyres can be dreadful on tarmac: they howl at speed, wander all over the road and wear very rapidly. The 'standard' wheel and tyre sizes originally fitted to these vehicles were 6.00–16 on 4½in-wide rims (88in) and 7.50–16 on 5½in rims (109in). Some late 88in Series IIIs left the factory with 205/80R16 radial tyres on 5½in rims. Beware of fitting tyres that are too large: anything over 7.50R16 or 235/85R16 is going to make the steering very heavy and can foul on the front springs on full

lock. Big wide tyres will also tend to float on the surface of the mud, rather than digging down to the harder ground beneath it.

There are two types of tyre construction: crossply and radial. Most Series II, IIA and III Land Rovers left the factory fitted with crossply tyres. These are now obsolete and increasingly hard to obtain. They tend to wander and 'tramline' more readily on rutted roads than the more modern radial tyres. They have a tall, narrow appearance, quite different from radials. Their size is measured in inches: 6.00–16 denotes a tyre 6in wide with a sidewall 6in tall, to fit a 16in-diameter wheel rim. The classic 'Avon Traction Mileage' crossply tyre is still available new in size 6.00–16, as are off-road-biased tyres with a heavy chevron-pattern tread, similar to the old Goodyear Xtra Grip once favoured by the military. This type of tyre is very noisy on tarmac at any speed above 30mph (48km/h) or so.

For a vehicle in daily use, radial tyres are probably a more sensible option, offering superior stability and wet weather road-grip. Most of these use a combination of imperial and metric measurements: 205/80R16 denotes a tyre 205mm wide, with a sidewall depth 80 per cent of the width (i.e. 164mm), to fit a 16in-rim. Some radial tyres intended for commercial vehicles still use the imperial measurement system, notably 7.50R16, which is a direct replacement for a 7.50–16 crossply tyre. Radial tyres are available with a wide variety of tread patterns, ranging from road-biased designs (good on tarmac, hard-wearing but tending to quickly become clogged in mud) to open-tread 'Mud Terrain' and even more aggressive off-road tyres, which will tend to be noisy and wear quickly on tarmac.

All utility Land Rovers, from the first 1948 Series One to the last Defenders, share the same wheel stud pattern and spacing. The plain steel wheels from later vehicles will fit any older Land Rover quite happily, using the original wheel nuts. These wheels were available in three widths: 4½in rims are very narrow and only suitable for 6.00–16 crossply tyres; 5½in rims are the most common, sometimes referred to as 'long-wheelbase rims', and they are suitable for 205/80R16 radial tyres and 7.50–16 radials or crossplies; 5½in rims made for Series III and later vehicles had a slightly

Avon Traction Mileage crossply on 4½in rim: fitted to most 88in Series vehicles at birth.

6.00–16 crossply with chevron tread pattern. This one is made in Turkey by Lassa.

Road-biased 205/80R16 tyre on 5½in steel rim.

Aggressive open-tread mud tyre on an aftermarket steel wheel.

Discovery steel wheel is plain and robust.

White eight-spoke steel wheel.

wider offset. Later Defenders left the factory with wheels that look identical to the earlier type, but are suitable for use with tubeless tyres. These are stamped 'Tubeless'; all other types of wheel must be fitted with inner tubes. Most of the older wheels are of riveted construction and will leak air if not fitted with tubes. Rims of 6½in are quite rare but are suitable for 235/85R16 and 235/70R16 tyres.

You might also find a vehicle fitted with early Discovery steel wheels. These are 7in wide, sturdily constructed, of plain appearance and designed for tubeless tyres. The 'Wolf' wheel is a heavy-duty steel wheel with perforated centre, 7in wide and designed for military use. It has a much thicker centre than the standard steel wheel and ideally needs longer wheel studs. Extended studs are available in M16 size for Series III hubs, but not for the older Series II/IIA type, which should not be fitted with Wolf rims. Alloy wheels on Series vehicles are quite unusual: the large, protruding central hub and drive flange in most cases prevent the fitting of original Land Rover wheels designed for the Discovery or Range Rover Classic. Aftermarket wheels are available in a variety of sizes and patterns; the most common on older Land Rovers being the white eight-spoke steel wheels originally made by Weller in the seventies and widely copied. You might also find a vehicle running on GKN five-slot alloy wheels with open centres: again these were very popular in the seventies. They need special sleeved wheel nuts and

are normally 15in diameter to take wide American-style tyres, most commonly 30–9.50R15 (30in overall diameter, 9½in wide, 15in rim).

Lighting

As standard these vehicles are usually fitted with 7in sealed beam headlamps, rated at 60W main beam and 45W dipped

Halogen headlamps above, original sealed beams below. They look very similar.

Halogen headlamps have separate bulbs, sealed beams must be replaced as a unit.

Original lights, such as these Lucas items, are much rarer and sometimes command high prices.

beam. Early Series IIs had Lucas 700 series headlamps with separate bulbs of only 45/40W rating. These tungsten filament headlamps cast a lovely warm yellow glow over an area extending about 10ft (3m) in front of the vehicle. As an aid to seeing in the dark, they are not especially useful.

The headlamp units can easily be replaced with H4 halogen headlamps, as found on the Defender. These are readily available new and are rated at 60/55W. Halogen bulbs are far more efficient than tungsten, so the improvement is rather greater than the difference in wattage would suggest. The H4 units will fit the headlight mountings in exactly the same way as the originals. On vehicles fitted with 700 series headlights, the wiring harnesses between lights and main loom will need to be changed. You may also find that the headlight bowl and mountings are in poor condition. On Series IIs, a few early and late IIAs and Series IIIs, these are industry-standard items and readily available. Most Series IIAs with the headlights between the wings have them attached to the radiator panel from behind, and this type of mounting is now very hard to find. It is possible to replace them with front-mounted bowls and chrome

ABOVE: Cheap and cheerful side and tail lights commonly found on Series vehicles.

LEFT: Vehicles built up to 1973 had these combined stop/tail/number plate/reflector units. Reproductions are available new.

trim rings, as found on the Series II and a number of other British cars, including the original Mini.

Higher wattage bulbs are available to fit H4 light units, but the existing wiring loom and dip switch will struggle to cope with anything more than the standard bulbs. If fitting uprated bulbs, the entire headlight wiring system must be replaced, using heavy-duty cable (20A minimum) and wiring the dipswitch through a relay, so that it only has to carry a small current. None of these vehicles have fuses in the headlight feed, so it is a good idea to incorporate fuses into your new wiring. At the very least, the main and dip beam circuits should each have their own fuse.

Auxiliary driving lights are another useful improvement for night driving, especially on minor rural roads: the front bumper makes a convenient mounting point. They must be wired to come on with the main beam headlights using a separate fused feed and relay, not simply spliced into the existing main beam feed. Most pre-1980 vehicles do not have a rear fog-light. Aftermarket units are readily available and should be wired via a switch and relay, so that they can only be operated when the headlights are on. Hazard warning flashers can be purchased as a complete kit, designed for universal fitment to older classic cars and easy to instal. A few later Series IIIs (and all 109 V8s) had reversing lights operated by a switch mounted on the bracket for the gear lever. The parts for a 'factory' reversing light installation tend to be hard to obtain, and most people simply wire up the reversing light to a switch on the dashboard, with a 'tell-tale' warning light to prevent it from being left on by mistake.

Side and tail lights of the 'Wipac' rounded pattern are cheap, but made from plastic and tend to deteriorate fairly quickly. The contacts corrode and the coloured lenses fade. Original lights, especially Sparto units, are rare and much sought after, so do not be too quick to throw them away and replace them with more modern ones. Pre-1973 vehicles used the stop/tail lights to illuminate the number plate, so if replacing these with later Wipac-style lights, you will need to fit a separate number plate light and rear reflectors.

OFF-ROAD PERFORMANCE

Even in absolutely standard form, these vehicles are spectacularly capable off road, with the choice of tyres and the skill of the driver being the only limiting factors. You need to think carefully about exactly what you want the vehicle to do before you start to throw shiny new parts at it. You should also remember that original, unmodified vehicles are becoming quite rare and prices are starting to reflect this. Twenty years ago, Series One Land Rovers were cheap and plentiful, and many were extensively modified for off-road use. A battered but usable Series One off-roader can still be picked up for a couple of thousand pounds but straight, original examples are now fetching ten times that. In time, prices for the later Series vehicles will probably follow the same trend.

Raising one of these vehicles on its suspension is not easy due to the nature of leaf springs with their fixed front mounting. Some people fit extended military-pattern shackles to the rear of the springs, which will give about an inch of lift, but these must be fitted in conjunction with wedges between the axles and springs, otherwise the axle drive flanges will not be parallel with those on the gearbox, which can cause severe propshaft vibration at speed. Parabolic springs tend to give about an extra inch of ride height compared to standard springs, and also offer better axle articulation to keep the wheels in contact with the ground on rough terrain. If you raise the suspension much above

Mud terrain tyres, spotlights and an electric winch on a 109 V8 truck cab.

Substantial roll cage with backstays in a Series One trials machine.

the standard factory height, it may be necessary to fit longer brake hoses so that they are not stretched on full suspension travel. You may also find that your propshafts have insufficient articulation to cope with the increased ride height, especially the rear propshaft on short-wheelbase vehicles. 'Wide yoke' propshafts are available to rectify this problem.

For deep wading, you will want to consider water-proofing the vehicle. A high-level snorkel intake is only of any use if the rest of the intake system is thoroughly sealed and waterproofed. All these vehicles, apart from the V8, use an oil-bath air-cleaner that is not at all waterproof and cannot be connected to a snorkel. Ignition systems can be sealed with rubber gaiters over the coil and distributor

Substantial steering guard on a Series IIA.

cap. Axle breathers should be replaced with the extended type. Before deep wading, remember to fit the wading plug to the bottom of the flywheel housing (unless you want a clutch full of muddy water) and take it out again when you have finished. An electric cooling fan (with an override switch allowing it to be turned off manually) will stop the entire engine bay being sprayed with water.

Inside the vehicle you will want more supportive seats with strong headrests, and three or four point harnesses for when you get over-ambitious and roll your Land Rover onto its roof. You should also fit a battery isolator switch in a position where you can still reach it while hanging upside-down in your harness. If you are going to be doing the kind of off-road driving where there is a risk of turning the vehicle upside-down, a rollover hoop is a must-have item. This should ideally pass through the rear body tub and be firmly anchored to the chassis, and should have diagonal backstays. Military Land Rover Defenders used a substantial hoop supported only by the cappings for the rear body tub. One of these can fairly easily be adapted to fit an older vehicle and offers reasonable protection, although it is unlikely to be acceptable for competition use.

Some underbody protection is also likely to be a good idea. The steering rods sit in front of the axle and are vulnerable to off-road damage. The differential pan on the front axle is also fairly weak and vulnerable, as is the bottom of the fuel tank. Heavy steel guards can be bought for all of these areas. Uprated steering rods, made of much larger diameter thick-wall tube, are also available. Steel rock sliders replace the decorative side sills and provide a good deal of protection, particularly on vehicles with underseat fuel tanks. They can also be obtained with projecting steel bars known as tree sliders. Chequer-plate panel protectors are generally more decorative than functional, but a pair of chequer-plate wing tops will provide a useful place to rest your tools when repairing your vehicle, and will also allow you to stand safely on the front wings.

Uprated drivetrain components (such as propshafts and halfshafts) for Series vehicles are quite rare. Several manufacturers have offered these in the past but they have not generally been a great commercial success. For the really serious off-roader, it is possible to have both front and rear differentials fitted with locking devices (usually operated by compressed air from a small auxiliary pump), which will maintain traction even when two diagonally opposed wheels are off the ground. Limited slip differentials serve the same purpose but do not need to be manually engaged.

For the most extreme off-road conditions, you might consider a winch. This will normally be an electrically operated drum winch, bolted to a specially made front bumper incorporating strong mounting points. If you are fitting a winch, you need to be sure that the front end of the chassis is rock solid: there have been instances where people have managed to pull the entire front end off the chassis when winching. Capstan winches were once a popular option on Series vehicles and were driven directly from the front of the engine. You might also come across a mechanical drum winch driven via a power take-off on the back of the transfer box. Mechanical winches have the advantage that they do not need electrical power. If you have an electric winch, you will probably want to fit a second battery to power it, along with a split charging system, so that you do not run the vehicle battery flat and find yourself unable to start the engine.

Military-pattern front bumper and custom-made winch mount firmly bolted to the front crossmember on this much-used trials vehicle.

A fair few Series vehicles still have a capstan winch at the front.

rebuilding a Land Rover

So you have this dream. You buy an old Land Rover Series II, IIA or III that has been asleep in a barn for a few years, tow it home and, over a few months, you bring it back to life. Looking at the prices being achieved at auction for 'barn find' restoration projects, you are not alone. Every year there must be hundreds, even thousands of old Land Rovers extracted from their last resting place and transported to a new home and (perhaps) a new life.

Equally, a quick scan through the classified ads will turn up plenty of abandoned restoration projects. 'All hard work done, just needs finishing' seems to be the most common selling pitch. Far more restorations are started than are ever finished and, sadly, a fair few of these project vehicles, having once escaped the scrap yard, end up being broken up anyway, as their would-be saviour desperately tries to recoup some of the thousands of pounds spent on parts.

TOP: … from this …

… via this …

… and this …

… and this …

… to this.

A sad sight: an abandoned restoration project. Do not let this happen to you.

So how do you avoid ending up in this position? There are many things you need to consider before taking on a project. Do you have the time, space, equipment and basic skills to do the job? Will your better half put up with you spending hours out in the garage working on 'that old heap' rather than redecorating the spare bedroom, which you promised to do three years ago? Will your finances stretch to cover the inevitable cost increases, as you discover that the engine block is frost-cracked, the gearbox will select every gear except top and the bulkhead has more glass-

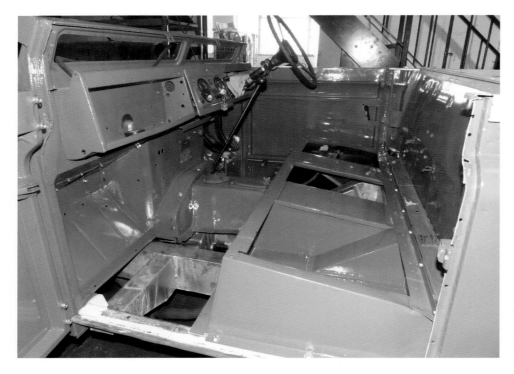

Bulkhead and seat box in place, but still a lot to do. Quite a few restorations get this far before running out of steam.

fibre in it than a Reliant Robin? Are you disciplined enough to dismantle the vehicle in an organized fashion, making notes and labelling parts as you go, or will you just pull the whole thing apart, throw the bits into old cardboard boxes and find, six months later, that you can't remember how it all goes back together? All these are reasons why projects fail, and you need to be really honest with yourself before getting into something that you might come to regret or even hate.

So let us assume you are in a position to restore a Land Rover and stand a good chance of actually getting it finished and running. At this point, the most important thing is to choose the right vehicle as a basis for your project. Far too many people start by finding an abandoned Land Rover and then decide that they will carry out a full restoration on that particular vehicle. That is entirely the wrong way round and almost bound to lead to trouble. For restoration projects, exactly the same rules apply as for any other vehicle purchase. Don't rush out and buy the first one you see, keep your options as open as possible and, above all, *do not fall in love with the vehicle*. Of course, if your whole motivation is to restore grandad's old Series II that he bought new in 1958 and you learned to drive in, none of the above applies, but if you just fancy restoring 'an old Land Rover', do yourself a favour and pick the right vehicle to start with.

So what are you looking for? First: completeness. Ideally you want a vehicle that is all in one piece with no significant bits missing. Even apparently minor items can be very hard to source, especially on early Series IIs, which are now nearly sixty years old. Avoid like the plague vehicles that have been partly or completely dismantled. You have no idea whether all the parts are there and, unless you have already rebuilt one of these vehicles, you will have a whole

lot of fun trying to work out which bits fit where. There are thousands of incorrect ways to assemble a Land Rover but only one correct one. If you try and guess how it all goes together, you will almost certainly guess wrong.

Second: originality. Ideally, you want a vehicle as unmolested as possible and largely as it left the factory. This will save you the dubious pleasure of trying to pick apart incomprehensible bodges made by previous owners. It also helps if the vehicle you are working on resembles, at least in major respects, the one in the workshop manual. All-original vehicles are an absolute joy to restore and the finished result will be far more authentic (and worth far more) than a 'bitsa' assembled from the best parts of ten or fifteen different vehicles.

Third: structural soundness. Many restorations start with a new galvanized chassis and, if this is the route you want to go down, then the condition of the chassis is unimportant. But if you have not budgeted for a new chassis, you had best check that the vehicle doesn't need one. Bulkhead condition is absolutely crucial – new bulkheads are very expensive indeed. There will almost certainly be some rot. Holes in footwells are easily fixed. Rotten door pillars are trickier, but not fatal. Serious rot along the top rail, round the fresh air vents or in the top inner corners, might well be too hard to repair, unless you are a welding genius or know someone who is. Even then, a bulkhead that rotten will have plenty more rot in places you can't see or get to.

Fourth: consider very carefully the condition of the rear body tub. Good, straight tubs are like hens' teeth. The tub is fabricated from spot-welded aluminium, which you will not be able to reproduce. It is possible to replace the wing skins using specialist panel adhesive (Sikaflex) and pop rivets, but it is not easy to keep the whole thing straight or to maintain the original strength. Holes in the floor are

Chassis replacement is not always needed. This Station Wagon has had a new bulkhead and doors, but the rest of the structure needed very little work.

This is why you should not store parts in cardboard boxes in a damp shed.

much maintenance in the couple of years before it was taken out of use. Expect all the mechanicals to be worn out and budget accordingly – anything less is a bonus. The good news is that it is all fixable (at a price).

Finally: beware of taking on a five-door 109 Station Wagon as a first project. They are magnificent, stately old beasts but pose some challenges not found on lesser vehicles. The main problem is that they have a fair bit of steel in the body structure (side frames, underfloor crossmembers). This rusts badly in itself and also corrodes the aluminium where the two metals meet. Putting right a rotten Station Wagon body can become a very expensive pastime. The second-row doors also corrode badly and are not cheap to replace. There are many people out there who have restored a Station Wagon successfully, but unless you really need one, you will be well advised to choose something simpler for your first restoration.

less of a problem, and the rear panels are much easier to replace than the sides, but a really battered, corroded and torn body tub will leave you hunting around for a better replacement, and you may need to look for some time.

Fifth: mechanical condition. People do not just tuck away old Land Rovers in barns for no good reason. If a vehicle has been taken out of use and dumped, it is usually either because the chassis has rotted beyond repair or because the vehicle has a major mechanical fault. Bear in mind also that an abandoned Land Rover is unlikely to have received

FACILITIES

Assuming that you are planning a full strip-down and rebuild onto a new chassis, what will you need to do the job? A fully dismantled Land Rover will take up at least three times the space of an intact one. You need to have

The restoration commences: stripping down a very rare 109 V8 High Capacity Pickup.

enough room to store all the parts, and to store them securely. Bits of Land Rover dumped on your driveway or in your front garden will attract scrap metal thieves and, sadly, there are many instances where vehicles under restoration have ended up being scrapped due to the theft of crucial components, such as the bulkhead or rear body tub. Although body panels will survive being left out in the open, mechanical parts, such as the engine and gearbox, should ideally be kept under cover.

Although it is possible to dismantle and reassemble a Land Rover in the open air, you will find you make far more rapid progress if you have a decent-sized garage to work in. Whether indoors or out, you will need a solid, concrete floor. If you do not have a garage, consider buying a large portable marquee to provide some shelter from the elements. You will also need to be able to call on a couple of friends to help you with the removal and refitting of some of the larger components, especially the roof, bulkhead and rear body tub.

Next, you will need suitable storage for all the parts you remove. Cardboard boxes are not suitable because when left in a damp garage they absorb moisture and anything left in them will corrode rapidly. You will need a good number of plastic storage boxes in a variety of sizes. For small components and assemblies, plastic freezer bags are ideal.

Tools – you will need to buy, hire or borrow an engine crane. A large (9in) disc cutter is also useful and will make short work of removing springs and cutting up the rotten chassis.

DISMANTLING

The key here is to break the vehicle down into easily handled sub-assemblies. Start by removing the detachable panels (doors, bonnet, tailgate), then the front wings, front panel, floors and transmission tunnel, seat box, roof and, finally, the rear body tub. You will then be able to lift the bulkhead off the chassis, crane out the engine and gearbox, and finally remove the axles. Try to avoid removing smaller components at this stage. For example, even if you plan to replace the doors, leave the old ones intact with hinges, check straps, latches and so on. It is far harder to misplace an entire door than a hinge, and if you remove small bits now, you may struggle to remember how they go back together in six or nine months' time.

If the chassis is to be replaced, do not waste too much time trying to undo rusty bolts. Use a disc cutter to slice through the tabs attaching the body tub to the chassis, ditto the bulkhead mounting bolts, underwing mudshields (unless perfect), exhaust system and anything else that you do not plan to reuse. Once you have the vehicle down to a bare, rolling chassis, you can support one end on a crane, lift the wheels slightly off the ground and cut straight through the springs just short of the hangers (assuming they are to be replaced, of course). Roll the axle out, cut through the 'U' bolts and remove the springs; place the chassis on stands and repeat with the other end. The chassis can then be cut up with the large disc cutter into pieces small enough to handle, and taken down to the nearest scrapyard along with the old springs.

By the time you have finished stripping your vehicle, you will be surprised how many bits you have to throw away.

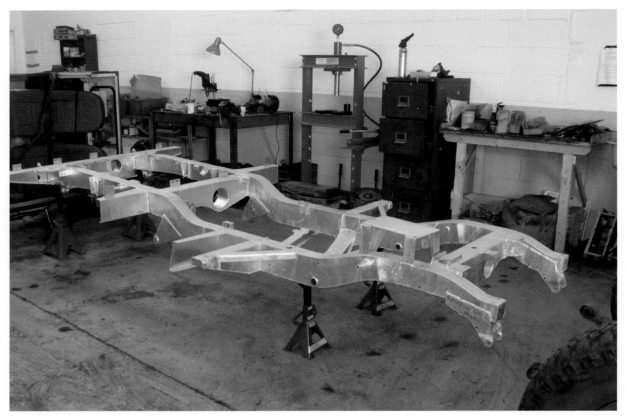

The heart of a full restoration: a new galvanized chassis.

THE NEW CHASSIS

Although the basic dimensions of Series II, IIA and III chassis did not change between 1958 and 1985, there are a number of small but significant differences. Brake hose mounting brackets, fuel tank position, centre crossmember and the mounts at the front of the rear body tub, all vary between early and late vehicles. It is possible to buy an original specification chassis for almost every variant of these vehicles, but there are also cheaper chassis on the market that are claimed to fit all models, but are invariably built to the Series III pattern. To fit one of these to an earlier vehicle, you will need to fit Series III brake hoses and brackets to the front axle, and re-drill the mounting holes at the front of the rear body tub. A long-wheelbase Series III chassis is also unlikely to have the supporting outrigger for the underseat fuel tank fitted to most earlier vehicles.

You should carefully inspect your new chassis, clean out any surplus galvanizing material from the various mounting holes and run a ¼in UNF thread tap up the four threaded holes under the steering relay mount to ensure the threads are clean. Whether or not you paint the chassis is up to you. Galvanized steel is notoriously difficult to paint, as ordinary primer and paint will not key to the surface and will start to flake off after a few months. Painting your chassis will help to keep the vehicle looking original, protect the galvanized finish from being worn away over time, and hopefully make the vehicle less attractive to thieves. If you decide to paint your chassis, it should first be treated with Mordant solution to etch the surface, then primed and painted (either by spray or brush) with a hard-wearing enamel as the top coat.

BULKHEAD

While the vehicle is in bits, it will normally make sense to cut all the corrosion out of the bulkhead and weld in new metal. Depending on the extent of the rot, you may need to strip the bulkhead bare, which is a time-consuming task, especially on a Series III. Make a careful note of what goes where, and retrieve all the small fittings, clips, brackets, etc., as some of these may be hard to replace. Stripping the bulkhead has the advantage that once repairs have been completed, the complete assembly can be given some kind of corrosion protection. The main methods used are galvanizing or hot zinc spraying.

Galvanizing will involve dipping the entire bulkhead in acid to remove all traces of old paint, oil, surface rust, etc., which might prevent the coating from adhering to the metal. The bulkhead is then immersed in a large vat of molten zinc: this bonds with the steel, providing a rust-proof surface that is 'self-healing', so that minor scratches in the surface do not result in rust developing. This treatment has the advantage that it penetrates (in theory) the internal box sections, but the heat involved can distort the bulkhead, in some cases badly enough to render it scrap. This applies especially to Series III bulkheads, which are made of rather thinner metal in places than the Series II/IIA type. Successful galvanizing requires a great deal of care and skill on the part of the operator.

For hot zinc spraying, the exterior surfaces of the bulkhead are sandblasted and then sprayed with molten zinc using a special spray gun that feeds zinc wire into the nozzle where it passes through an electric arc. This is a

To cut out all the rot from a bulkhead, drastic surgery is sometimes needed.

much gentler process, which does not heat and distort the steel: it creates a tough but coarsely textured zinc coating that will require several thick coats of filler/primer before it is smooth enough to paint. The process is generally cheaper than galvanizing and can be extended to other steel components, such as bulkhead supports, seatbelt brackets and even the door and bonnet frames. As the zinc spray does not penetrate hollow box sections, such as door pillars, these must be treated with a wax-based corrosion inhibitor such as Waxoyl.

For a really top-class restoration, new bulkheads are now available from Pegasus for all Series II and IIA models, with Series III bulkheads expected to be available shortly; these reproduce the originals in every detail. They are not cheap, but a vehicle rebuilt around a new galvanized chassis and bulkhead should in theory last forever.

FASTENERS

The bodywork on these vehicles was generally held together with UNF fasteners in a fairly small number of sizes. You will find that metric fasteners can be substituted and are far cheaper and easier to obtain than UNF. Stainless-steel fasteners might seem like a good idea but have their disadvantages: they are far more expensive that zinc-plated mild steel, rather less strong and have a nasty habit of seizing if the threads become contaminated with dirt. They are also almost impossible to drill out. Stainless steel should never be used for structurally critical areas, such as steering, suspension or braking components, tow hitch mounts or engine and gearbox mountings.

Rather than trying to reuse rusty old fasteners, it is far better to go to your nearest nut and bolt stockist and purchase new ones in quantity. The table provides sizes that will cover most of the parts that you need. Form 'C' washers are thicker and a larger diameter than Form 'A'.

Fastener sizes			
Fastener type	Diameter	Length (mm)	Quantity
Hex head set screw	M5	16	50
	M6	20	100
	M8	20	100
	M8	30	50
	M10	30	20
Spring washer	M5		50
	M6		100
	M8		150
	M10		20
Form 'A' washer	M5		100
	M6		100
	M8		100
Form 'C' washer	M6		200
	M8		200
	M10		50
Repair washer	M6		50
	M8		50

MECHANICAL OVERHAUL

If your vehicle was running and drivable before you started dismantling it, you should have a fair idea of what will need to be done. If not, you will have to take a view on how far you go with stripping and overhauling mechanical components. There are some jobs that are far, far easier to do while the vehicle is apart. Items you should almost certainly be looking at include:

◆ Replace the front and rear crankshaft oil seals on the engine.
◆ Replace the timing chain and reset the pump timing (2.25 diesel).

Consumable components, such as brakes, will normally be replaced as a matter of course.

- Replace the clutch.
- Strip the main gearbox and replace worn or broken parts, as required.
- Replace the sector shaft oil seal in the steering box.
- Replace all the steering rod joints and especially the ones on the longitudinal arm between the steering box and relay. Note that these joints must not be the type with grease nipples, as clearance is very tight.

Axles tend to be easier to work on once they are attached to the vehicle, unless the casings need welding work. Provided that they appear sound, turn freely and do not have too much free play in them, the internals can usually be left alone until the vehicle is back on the road.

PAINTING

If you plan to repaint your vehicle, it will be much better to do it while the body is in bits, not least because there will be far less masking-off required. This is how the vehicles

Panels are best painted individually. This is a wing for a 1960 Series II.

were painted at the factory. The type of finish you use will depend on your facilities and budget. For spray painting, old-fashioned cellulose paint is by far the most forgiving for the amateur. It dries almost instantly, imperfections can easily be sanded or polished out and it is fairly inexpensive, although now only available from a few specialist suppliers. Synthetic enamel is much harder to spray: it is very slow-drying and tends to sag and run if applied slightly too thickly. It takes several weeks to harden properly and trying to sand down blemishes before the paint has fully set will just result in a sticky mess. Modern 'two pack' paint uses a cyanide-based hardener, and if you try to spray this without the correct breathing apparatus, you are likely to end up dead.

Brush or roller painting can achieve a good result with patience. You need very high-quality brushes, and the paint should be warmed before use by standing it in a bath of hot water. Synthetic brushing enamel or 'coach paint' has all the same disadvantages as the spray-applied version. Light colours tend to show up brush marks less readily than dark ones.

Bare aluminium must be primed using a special etch primer, otherwise your new paint will fall off in sheets. Etch primer is available in aerosols or in tins for spraying. You need to be aware also that cellulose primer and paint cannot be applied over old enamel paint: it will react and crinkle up. It can be sprayed over the paint originally used by Land Rover, but if the vehicle has previously been repainted, you will probably need to either take it back to bare aluminium (which takes forever) or apply a coat of special barrier primer first. Minor body imperfections can be filled and sanded before priming, but make sure you use a flexible filler. Large dents (especially on the wings) will really need beating flat, as these panels flex a lot in service and even flexible filler is likely to crack and fall out if applied over a large area.

REASSEMBLY

The usual procedure is to fit the axles and springs first, then the engine, gearbox, steering relay, track rod, drag link and propshafts to give you a rolling chassis. The spring shackle pins should not be tightened at this stage, and it is unlikely that you will be able to fit the shock absorbers until the body is back on the chassis, as there will not be enough weight to compress the springs. The next stage will be to fit all the rigid and flexible brake pipes and unions, and to thread the rear wiring loom through the chassis. This can be done by feeding a long length of stiff fencing wire through from back to front, bending over the front end, taping the back end of the new loom to the wire and carefully drawing the wire back out of the chassis bringing the loom with it. Finally, you can fit the steering relay, not forgetting the lower clamp ring that bolts to the crossmember, and the track rod and drag link.

Rear body tub next, as this is a fixed item with no room for adjustment. Bolt it to the tabs at the back of the chassis, but leave the front end unbolted for now. The rear tub will act as a datum point for the alignment of the bulkhead, which is possibly the most critical part of the entire build. The bulkhead must be perfectly vertical, with a distance of 34½in (876mm) between the rear face of the door pillars and the front edge of the body tub, on both sides. The position of the bulkhead is adjusted via slotted vertical holes where the uprights mount to the footwells, horizontally slotted holes where the uprights attach to the chassis and spacing washers, as required, between the bulkhead mounting feet and the chassis outriggers. Once you think you have the bulkhead in the right place, run a piece of string along the crease line at the top of the curve on the body tub and check that this crease lines up with the corresponding crease in the door pillar. It is quite common for rear tubs to collapse slightly at the front end with age, and if the door pillars and body tub do not line up, the doors will not fit properly. The front end of the tub can be raised slightly, if required, by inserting packing pieces in between the floor crossmembers and the mounting pads on the chassis. Rear axle check straps make an ideal packing material: they can be cut into small sections and glued in place. Then recheck the door gaps and trial-fit the doors. You should find that you can achieve a nice, even gap at both front and rear door edges, and a straight crease line all the way along the side of the vehicle. Once you have this bit right, you can remove the doors and continue putting your Land Rover back together.

Body tub and bulkhead in place, bolts left loose until the doors have been trial-fitted.

Up and running, but with quite a few bits still to bolt on. If you reach this point, you will probably be able to get your project finished.

Every panel visible here has been painted separately …

Once the front wings and radiator panel are in place, leave the bolts between the wings and panel loose, and try to fit the bonnet. There is a fair amount of fore and aft adjustment on the radiator panel, and if you get the positioning too far out, the striker pin on the lower front edge of the bonnet will not engage with the bonnet catch. The catch itself can be moved slightly after loosening the two mounting bolts, but the amount of adjustment is limited. When finally tightening the wing bolts, make sure the tops of both wings are level with each other.

Always use plain washers and spring washers when assembling bodywork. Plain nuts without spring washers will vibrate loose and Nylocs will make any subsequent dismantling much harder than it needs to be. There are a couple of exceptions: Nylocs should be used for the front lower edge of the radiator panel, and where the bulkhead support uprights bolt to the footwells.

FINAL ASSEMBLY AND DETAILING

Restorations are often let down by poor attention to detail.

If you want your Land Rover to give long and reliable service, it is well worth taking the time to ensure that everything is assembled correctly, using, wherever possible, the same materials and methods that were employed by the factory. Rubber seals (doors, fresh air vents, steering column) should be replaced with new. Wiring should be carefully routed to avoid rubbing and secured with appropriate clips, not just lashed to the nearest available component with cable ties. Floor panels should be sealed with mastic around the edges, so that they do not leak or rattle. Door hinges and catches need to be in good condition (replacements are inexpensive) and carefully adjusted so that the doors close easily and do not pop open on bumpy roads. The exhaust system should be hung correctly, using the original type of mountings, and routed so that it does not rattle against the chassis or gearbox. Your aim should be to build a vehicle which feels 'tight' and well screwed together: do this and you will truly have a Land Rover for life.

A final word of warning: rebuilding Land Rovers is addictive. Once you have your vehicle back on the road, you may soon find yourself looking for another one to restore.

Interior of a newly-restored Series II. Seat belts are the only obvious concession to modernity.

Alpine lights   Narrow oval windows to be found in the outer edges of the roof on *Station Wagons*. Sometimes fitted as an optional extra on hard-top vehicles.

Bulkhead   The structure between the engine bay and vehicle interior, to which the windscreen, front doors, front wings and bonnet are attached. Made of mild steel and can rot badly. Very expensive to replace.

Bull bar   Large piece of ironmongery bolted to the front bumper for added crash protection. Now rather unfashionable as they are not very pedestrian-friendly.

Cat flap   Popular term for the top-hinged upper tailgate found on some *hard-top* vehicles.

Centre differential   Found in the *transfer box* on 109 V8 models. Allows permanent four-wheel drive without excessive tyre wear. Can be locked for off-road use in slippery conditions.

Chequer plate   Shiny 3mm aluminium sheet with an 'anti-slip' pattern. Intended for use on gangways, ramps, etc., but hugely fashionable for giving Land Rovers that tough, industrial look. Now available in a huge variety of pre-cut shapes to attach to almost every inner and outer surface of your Land Rover. Handy for covering up minor damage to wings, sills, etc., but otherwise purely decorative.

Chrome balls   See *steering swivels*.

County   'Luxury' trim specification, found on late Series III *Station Wagons*. Cloth seats, headlining and tinted windows.

Differential   Big, heavy lump of ironmongery found in the middle of each axle. Takes the drive from the *transfer box* and transmits it to the wheels, allowing them to rotate at slightly different speeds to compensate for uneven surfaces.

Double-declutching   Driving technique which allows crunch-free gear changes on gearboxes with no (or badly worn) *synchromesh*. Essential for Series II/IIA drivers, useful on Series IIIs with worn gearboxes.

EP90   Heavy-duty gear oil, used in the gearbox, *transfer box*, axles and *steering swivels*. The stuff that leaks onto your drive.

Free-wheeling hubs   Popular accessory for Series' vehicles, disconnects the front wheels from the front differential and driveshaft to reduce drag, noise and vibration when running on-road in two-wheel drive.

Hard top   Van-type body, usually comes with a *safari door*. Can be fitted with side-windows and rear seats.

Hood sticks   The metal framework that supports a canvas roof.

Outriggers   Structural steel extensions welded to the outside of the main chassis rails, providing support for the tub, bulkhead and fuel tanks.

Overdrive   Highly desirable accessory for Series' vehicles, effectively adds a fifth gear for relaxed cruising.

Parabolic springs   Specially shaped leaf springs, which replace the original 'cart springs', giving a softer ride and better axle articulation.

Rag top   Popular term for a full-length canvas roof.

Safari door   Full-depth, side-opening rear door. Standard on all *Station Wagons*, optional (although very common) on other hard-top Series' vehicles.

Salisbury axle   A heavy-duty rear axle, fitted to long-wheelbase Series III vehicles. Can be fitted to earlier long-wheelbase vehicles, but requires expert welding to adapt for short-wheelbase ones. Almost indestructible and therefore highly desirable.

Seat box   Hollow aluminium box-shaped structure that supports the seats. Can be removed for easier access to the gearbox.

Stage One   The unofficial name given to the 109 V8, an interim model, which had most of the features of the Series III, but permanent four-wheel drive and a V8 engine, and introduced the flat front design that became standard on the 90/110 and Defender.

Station Wagon   The original people carrier. Short-wheelbase vehicles seat seven; long-wheelbase vehicles seat ten or twelve, depending on specification. Rear seats are cramped and uncomfortable for adults but brilliant for children.

Steering swivels   To be found at each end of the front axle. They contain the driveshaft joints, which run in a bath of *EP90*. The oil is prevented from leaking out by a rubber seal around a large chrome ball. The chrome becomes pitted and rusty, the seal tears and you get oil leaks. Replacing chrome balls is an involved and expensive job.

Synchromesh   The system that allows smooth, crunch-free gear changes. Taken for granted on modern cars, but

Series II and IIA vehicles only had synchromesh on third and fourth gears. The mechanism can wear badly, resulting in crunchy gear changes. These can be avoided by *double-declutching*.

Three-quarter canvas   A canvas roof that covers only the rear load area, fitted in conjunction with a *truck cab*.

Transfer box   A two-speed gearbox that sits behind the main gearbox and transfers the drive to the front and rear wheels.

Truck cab   A short, hard roof that just covers the front seats, allowing the vehicle to be used as a pickup truck.

Tub (or body tub)   Rear body section; a single-piece item from the rear of the doors to the tailgate.

Two and a quarter (or 2.25)   Popular term for the 2286cc 4-cylinder engine, either petrol or diesel.

appendix: basic service data

Engine type	2286cc petrol	2286cc petrol	2625cc petrol	2625cc petrol	3528cc petrol	2286cc diesel
Compression ratio	7:1	8:1	7:1	7.8:1	8.13:1	23:1
Spark plug gap (mm)	0.75–0.80	0.75–0.80	0.75–0.80	0.75–0.80	0.80	N/A
Points gap (mm)	0.35–0.40	0.35–0.40	0.35–0.40	0.35–0.40	0.35–0.40	N/A
Timing (static)	3 degrees BTDC	TDC	2 degrees BTDC	2 degrees ATDC	TDC	N/A
Valve clearances (mm) (engine hot)	Inlet 0.25 Exhaust 0.25	Inlet 0.25 Exhaust 0.25	Inlet 0.15 Exhaust 0.25	Inlet 0.15 Exhaust 0.25	Self-adjusting	Inlet 0.25 Exhaust 0.25
Firing order	1-3-4-2	1-3-4-2	1-5-3-6-2-4	1-5-3-6-2-4	1-8-4-3-6-5-7-2	1-3-4-2

Note: timing settings are those quoted by the manufacturer for running on fuel of a far lower octane rating than the minimum available in the United Kingdom. When running on 95 octane fuel, it is usually possible to advance the timing by around six degrees from the figures given without ill effects.

index